Automatic Controls for Heating and Air Conditioning

Automatic Controls for Heating and Air Conditioning: Pneumatic-Electric Control Systems

Harry J. Edwards, Jr.

McGraw-Hill Book Company

New York   St. Louis   San Francisco   Auckland
Bogotá   Hamburg   Johannesburg   London
Madrid   Mexico   Montreal   New Delhi
Panama   Paris   São Paulo   Singapore
Sydney   Tokyo   Toronto

Library of Congress Cataloging in Publication Data

Edwards, Harry J
   Automatic controls for heating & air conditioning

   Includes index.
1. Heating—control.   2. Ventilation—control.
3. Air conditioning—control.   4. Pneumatic control.
5. Temperature control.   I. Title.
TH7466.5.E38   697   79-22828
ISBN   0-07-019046-1

   34567890   KPKP   898765432

The editors for this book were Jeremy Robinson and Joan
Matthews; the designer was Mark E. Safran, and the
production supervisor was Sally Fliess. It was set in
Baskerville by Bi-Comp, Incorporated.

It was printed and bound by The Kingsport Press.

Contents

Contents

List
of
Figures

List of Figures

Preface

The air conditioning industry has made tremendous strides in applying technology over the past two decades. Improvements in performance have been coupled with greater efficiency in equipment, and engineering practices have been refined until we now have a broad base of sound criteria to call upon at the outset of any airconditioning design project. And engineering societies, seminars, and formal educational offerings will continue to dedicate themselves to further research and development aimed at better environmental comfort at lower costs.

The control industry has kept pace, and today, in accordance with demands for operational economies, controls and their applications are slanted toward building comfort with the greatest economies possible. "Free cooling," or the utilization of outdoor air for cooling, when outdoor air temperatures are suitable, helps building owners hold off startup of mechanical cooling equipment until absolutely necessary. Night setback, or lowering of space temperatures during unoccupied periods, assists in the conservation of fuel required for the generation of heat. And energy monitoring and load shedding offer even greater savings through priority shutdown of equipment before new demand peaks are set, which often frequently establish the billing rate a customer pays for electricity.

Pneumatic temperature controls have progressed from the predominant use of remote bulb instruments of not so many years ago to temperature transmitters, which report to controllers located in control panels where conditions are more easily refined through careful adjustments and where temperature readouts can be conveniently grouped to aid in temperature-management decisions. And development of devices that use less compressed air has contributed, if only slightly, to conservation of electrical energy required at the air compressor. Of course, dual-temperature day-night thermostats permit setting back temperatures at night, with selective local override for areas which must be occupied during nights or weekends.

Applications themselves, too, have introduced economies to help hold down building operating costs, particularly those related to heating and cooling. Careful consideration is routinely given, now, to outdoor air, not just using it when it is right for cooling but also not using too much when outside air temperatures are low, as the introduction of too much fresh air can impose additional heating loads on the building's heat generating equipment. Larger systems will often employ terminal units under control of thermostats, which can vary air flow requirements downward as the cooling load falls off, allowing fan energy requirements to be throttled through the use of fan capacity controls.

With the emphasis expected to continue through the years on comfort with conservation, system designers will be more cognizant than ever of the need to evaluate applications on the basis of practicality, performance, and economy. Control system designers will need good grassroots education in the basics of device and system operation, as well as air conditioning theory. Those of us in the field must look to the development of future application engineers and be ready to assist in the perpetuation of qualified personnel by giving of our time and talents in the area of education.

The following chapters of this book will try to deal with pneumatic temperature controls, as to why we need them, what they are, how they work, how they are applied, and what to look for in terms of performance. Peripheral matters closely related to temperature controls are covered, too, such as the equipment that they are used on, accessories, control wiring, and motor starters. In all cases, I hope that the matters covered here are in harmony with the best strandard practices and good engineering judgment.

Please note that all temperatures cited throughout this book are in degrees Fahrenheit. Also, limitations of our language being what they are, masculine nouns and pronouns need to be read in the purely generic sense, and are intended to refcr both to men and women. I hope my readers will read them in this context, as no limitation is intended.

Harry J. Edwards, Jr.

Acknowledgments

The best part of a good thing is sharing it with others. That is what I have tried to do in writing this book on pneumatic temperature controls. It has been my good fortune to have spent the past fifteen years working in the temperature control field, and even today, I continue to be fascinated with the applications and many varying techniques to be exploited in this exciting and challenging field.

Frustrations abound when trying to write a book that will cover such a broad field as temperature controls. It is hoped that the reader will forgive any shortcomings in this text, which has attempted to tackle a highly specialized engineering technology.

For years, courses on the subject of pneumatic temperature controls have called upon the teacher's resourcefulness in the preparation of teaching materials and student reference aids. Manufacturers of controls have contributed generously and effectively with good teaching aids, and if not for them, there would have been many areas with little or no adequate information. A definitive outline has not been universally accepted, and so it may have been difficult to establish a firm uniformity in the offerings of classes on this subject. This book is offered as a candidate for use in any educational experience that attempts to deal with the subject.

My sincerest thanks go to my encouragers and proofreaders and to my family who kept me from feeling too guilty over the time I took from them for this work. And a very special thanks to the industry that supported us and our young ones through their growing up years, the industry of automatic temperature controls.

Introduction

Pneumatic temperature controls are found in commercial and industrial heating and air conditioning work. Their use is justified by cost savings over electric or electronic systems, when (1) the temperature controls need to be modulating in nature, and (2) the savings of installing air piping over electrical wiring are enough to offset the cost of furnishing and wiring an air compressor, depending on the size of the control system. This point is frequently reached when control requirements call for two dozen or more control devices, consisting of thermostats, valves, relays, or damper actuators. Many systems in larger buildings will utilize hundreds of devices, and some, in buildings of significant size, can mean control devices numbering into the thousands. A simple pneumatic tube, instead of multiple wires in conduit, can mean real savings in construction costs when many areas requiring temperature control are involved.

Pneumatic controls are proportioning. Gradually increasing and decreasing air signals that relate to temperature demands of conditioned spaces are easily used to modulate control valves regulating flow or dampers regulating air quantities. They lend themselves nicely to introducing changes in temperature on a gradual basis. And this is important in areas which must have substantial air flow in order to affect space conditioning, when sudden temperature changes would be noticeable and unacceptable.

In many areas of laboratory buildings, textile mills, and furniture factories, any electrical equipment must be explosion-proof. This introduces significant cost increases to temperature control work done electrically but poses no such problem for pneumatic controls, which are incapable of producing potentially hazardous arcing. This means that the same pneumatic controls can be utilized in all areas of a building, without regard to electrical safety requirements in areas needing explosion-proof devices.

Even where mechanical protection for polyethelene air piping is required, our raceway can make use of the quicker, easier-to-use raceway fittings, which often are prohibited by specifications for electrical work. And where rigid steel conduit is mandatory, real savings are apparent when electrical metallic tubing can be employed, instead, for our air piping raceway. Under such a specification, the miscellaneous electrical connections required to tie in our pneumatic system to any electrical equipment under control can be minimized by placement of the interface device close to the equipment it serves and making longer runs pneumatically.

Today, economies are more distinct than ever, as instrument-grade polyethelene tubing finds ever-increasing use, with exceptional success. Above lift-out ceilings, this tubing quite often can be run exposed, neatly installed and properly supported, at great savings over electrical installations, which necessitate conduit and wiring, and, with construction costs steadily rising, pneumatic controls will continue to enjoy regular usage.

From an owner's standpoint after the fact, the simplicity of operation of a pneumatic controller or actuator helps to keep a rein on maintenance costs. Essentially, they are temperature-actuated air regulators operating air-operated actuators with no concern for voltage or electrical safety during checkout and inspection. The devices themselves are relatively maintenance-free, and most make use of inlet air filters, to keep the instrument internally clean. Manufacturers offer replacement filters which can be changed at three- or four-year intervals, allowing owners to perpetuate reliable performance from their pneumatic controllers.

And, not to be overlooked, all major manufacturers offer regular, planned maintenance programs for pneumatic control systems. The manufacturer of a control system can make the installation and provide continuing service, as well, all with the goal of making pneumatic temperature controls the best buy for today's building owners.

Automatic Controls
for
Heating
and
Air Conditioning

Necessity for Automatic Systems

DIVERSE INTRABUILDING SITUATIONS

The modern day job-production requirements of American workers require that they be equipped with an environment that will be conducive to their making the best contribution they can toward the objective of their employer. In an office, in a factory, in a hospital, or even in a classroom, the best that individuals have to offer will more likely come forth if they are placed in an environment which does not create a hardship by imposing uncomfortable temperatures or relative humidity. It is for this reason that today's buildings must provide environmental flexibility to serve different types of occupants who have varying demands for heating or cooling.

Within any given building, the loads, in terms of heat generated by people and equipment which must be removed, will vary from area to area because of activities which may differ widely from one tenant to another.

Weather plays an extremely important role in terms of personal comfort, and the effects of weather cannot be ignored within a structure which houses many people both in summer and winter. In the summertime, the environmental system must be able to provide the necessary cooling to make the various areas suitable and comfortable. In the wintertime, the system must produce just enough heat, not too much, to make the areas comfortable for the various people within. Consider a multistory building with four of its sides exposed and the central areas on the various floors more or less protected from the perimeter by the occupied spaces in between (Figure 1).

People who have their offices around the perimeter of the building with an exposure to the outside wall of the building in the wintertime will feel colder because of the heat lost to the outside wall which is the only

1

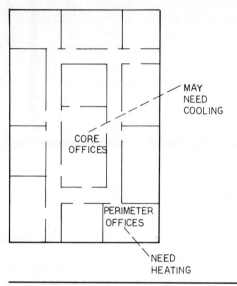

Figure 1   A typical floor of a multistory building, at 30 degrees outside.

barrier between them, their environmental system, and the outside air. Their areas will require heat and will make demands on the environmental system to supply them with the necessary heat to ensure comfort, while offsetting the heat losses to the outside. Conversely, those who are on the inside may very well have a need for some cooling from the environmental system, owing to the fact that they are insulated, as it were, from the outside walls by the other conditioned areas and their occupants. Were we to try to determine air-conditioning needs for the entire floor based on conditions in either the central or perimeter areas, we would find difficulty in satisfying the temperature requirements for one group or the other, because when we applied heat generally to the area to satisfy the demands of those closer to the outside wall we would find that those situated on the inside were too warm. Conversely, were we to introduce cooling generally, based on demands from the interior zones, to allieviate the heat load that the interior-zone sensors were saying was there, we would soon find that those on the perimeter would suffer from being too cool. These conflicting situations point up the need for some form of automatic response to the different areas, based on localized conditions and the ability to deal with area heat gains and heat losses on an individual basis.

An additional consideration as we look at the intrabuilding situation, has to do with a room which is occupied only part of the time. On the perimeter of a building, with no people in the room, it is obvious that the room would become cool, requiring heat. But as soon as the people gather who normally use the room, say a meeting area, we have a load now generating heat of its own, and an automatic response is required which will shut off the heat being delivered to that area, as soon as it is sensed that the heat load of the people now in the room is making the heretofore set amount of heat unnecessary. We must now provide some automatic form of heat reduction and perhaps even cooling, or within a short time, the crowd will begin to feel uncomfortably warm.

Assuming that our readers are already familiar with heat loads from various sources, we won't attempt to discuss the thermodynamics of heat generation by people gathered in an area and the fact that people have a certain Btu output of their own that varies with their activity.

TENANT DEMANDS

In today's competitive atmosphere, particularly as pertains to the leasing of space for use in the conduct of business, we find we have a mandate to deliver a comfortable environment to those who would be our tenants. It is an ordinary situation now to find buildings that offer heating and/or cooling on a year-round basis, with the needed flexibility to handle thermal conditions likely to arise. When we have tenants approach a landlord, we have people who are expecting flexible environmental systems which will make them comfortable without their having to worry about making decisions as to whether they need heating or cooling.

The modern tenant is a very basic motivation toward providing space conditioning which incorporates automatic controls to deal with temperature developments. We soon see that a building's owner cannot afford to be without automatic systems that will guarantee to his tenants the comfort they have a right to expect and will guarantee to the building owner that he won't experience difficulty in leasing his spaces because of uncomfortable conditions. It is unreasonable to expect that anyone will remain in an environment which is not conducive to their carrying on their business when they are paying good money for the space they have leased.

ENERGY COSTS

When we look into energy costs for any given building, we can quickly grasp an understanding of the need for automatic systems. With the costs of manufacturing energy and energy resources rising rapidly, we now must have automatic systems that not only provide comfort but that do it as economically as possible. Strikes connected with the production of energy-source raw materials concern everyone greatly, particularly when they are of any significant duration. Strikes spotlight the fact that consumption of energy is ever increasing, and the vitality of our nation is dependent upon uninterrupted production of energy material. It is reasonable to expect that energy costs will continue to rise as larger wage settlements and spiraling equipment costs are incorporated in pricing which is ultimately passed on to consumers. Therefore, buildings, in order to be affordable from operational and maintenance standpoints, must utilize energy as economically and as prudently as possible. Automatic controls have a big role to play here, ranging from energy-saving thermostats, which lower space temperatures at night in the winter, to demand conscious controls, which monitor the amount of energy a building is using and shed loads on a priority basis in order to prevent establishing new peak demand levels which often set billing rates. Our considerations of building automatic controls will be centered primarily upon diverse intrabuilding temperature situations and how we go about handling them.

2

System Classifications

Two broad classifications of modes of automatic control have long been established in earlier manuals, but they bear repeating here to point out their basic differences.

TWO-POSITION CONTROL

This mode is basically snap-acting in nature. The device responds to a temperature change or pressure change and does so by making a definite movement. The thermostat in a typical residence on a fall in temperature closes its contacts, which energizes the burner. On a temperature rise, when the thermostat is satisfied, the contacts open, and the burner shuts down. We call this "two-position" control because it is either full on or full off. There is no in between in terms of calling upon system capacities. The ordinary residential thermostat is a good illustration of single-stage, two-position control. This can be expanded by the addition of more stages.

If we add additional steps to utilize part or all of system capacity, we have multistage, two-position control, where each of the stages acts independently, depending on the severity of temperature deviation from the setpoint, to bring on its respective portion of the system being controlled. Heat pumps are a good example of a system that utilizes multistage, two-position thermostats. Many residential units incorporate supplemental electric strip heaters which are energized by a second heating stage when heating demands can no longer be met by the reversed refrigerant cycle during extremely cold, and less efficient, outdoor air temperatures.

Two-position, multistage thermostats are frequently used in connection with duct heaters in reheat systems, where the duct heaters serve individual offices or areas, and the electric heater element is divided into

5

several stages, so that the heater may be stepped on in a gradual manner to add heat incrementally (see Figure 2). On a fall in space temperature severe enough to energize, say, all three stages, the respective contacts close in sequence until the heater is operating at full capacity. On a rise in temperature, the contacts open in reverse order, one at a time, each deenergizing its respective section of the heater until the heater is completely off as a result of rising or satisfied space temperatures.

One of the difficulties with two-position control is that frequently it keeps the equipment energized for too long a time. Consider a house which utilizes hot-water radiation heat. When the space is cold, the burner may come on and heat the water which will rise by convection to displace the colder water in the radiators. The thermostat will keep the burner going until it is satisfied. At that time, it will shut down the burner, but the flywheel effect within the system, or the thermal mass residual in the system which has been going full blast up until a moment ago, is enough to cause the heat output to continue beyond the requirements of the thermostat, and some overshoot in terms of space temperature will occur. This is easily understood when we consider the mass of radiators, how warm they get, and how long it takes for them to dissipate their heat once the burner is shut down.

To compensate for this, two-position control devices frequently incorporate an anticipator which, on a call for heat, applies false heat to the thermostat's sensing element, causing it to shut down the burner somewhat prematurely. This then allows the system to coast long enough to satisfy space requirements and to take advantage of the system lag or flywheel effect to permit the space temperatures to rise more gradually to thermostat setpoint before falling back again to where a new cycle will be initiated.

But even the utilization of an anticipator does not alter the fact that we still have basically a two-position device, that causes the system to operate

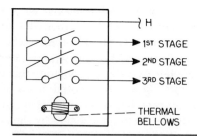

Figure 2   Two-position multistage heating thermostat. A continuing fall in temperature closes first- through third-stage contacts in sequence.

at full capacity for a short period of time and to shut down completely. In many environmental situations with variations in activities and loads within the conditioned spaces, when thermal flexibility is absolutely necessary, it is not sufficient to have a two-position control which swings from full on to full off. In this area, we would apply a mode of control which sees a deviation from setpoint and begins to take gradual action to correct it.

PROPORTIONAL CONTROL

Looking now into a mode of control which introduces the flexibility we need, we find proportional or modulating control, which is the second of our two broad classifications of systems. It has the ability to match system output with space demands. It allows us to take advantage of continuously operating systems by graduating or varying their output or by shutting them down completely if they are not needed. In this manner, we can eliminate the peaks and valleys of environmental temperature control experienced when pure two-position control is used alone.

A proportional controller, on a fall in space temperature, would begin to apply heat to the area on a gradual basis, perhaps by opening a heating hot water supply valve only far enough to introduce sufficient amount of water to warm the radiators or fin-tube radiation just enough to effect a slight rise in space temperature. Upon sensing this slight rise, the proportional controller would then reverse its action and cause the heating valve to move toward the closed position, perhaps all the way, but enough to diminish the flow of hot water in order to cause a drop in fin-tube or radiator output. This is accomplished by controls which respond on a gradual basis to the amount of demand being made on them by space temperature, and they may be electric, electronic, or pneumatic.

It is the proportional control mode that is used almost exclusively in commercial temperature control applications, because of its flexibility and because of its inherent capabilities to proportion the output of systems in an economic manner more consistent with space temperature demands. It is this area of control, and in particular these controls as they are applied pneumatically, with which later chapters of this book will deal.

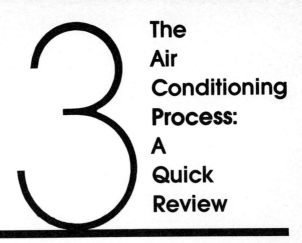

The Air Conditioning Process: A Quick Review

BASIC AIR HANDLER TYPES

The predominant piece of equipment in building air conditioning systems is the air handler, usually consisting of fan, filters, dampers, and cooling and heating coils (Figure 3). Generally, they are strategically located in larger buildings so that the ductwork which extends from them can be routed as economically as possible to the areas they serve. These units process the air returned to them, mix in some fresh air, and return it, thermally reconditioned, to the spaces served to serve again in providing heating or cooling as the space may demand. It is these air handlers that we will look at now, because these units very much utilize temperature controls, both space and unit-mounted, to tell them what temperature control job is required.

CENTRAL-STATION UNITS

For any given area, if space conditioning is to be accomplished by processing the air at a central location, central-station equipment is generally employed, where treatment of the air is handled, and then returned through ductwork to the conditioned spaces. These units are located in what is generally referred to as a fan room, and hot water for heating or chilled water for cooling may be piped from a remote boiler or chiller into the fan room where it will be introduced into water coils within the air handler for air treatment.

   Draw-through units have the blower positioned on the discharge side of the unit, arranged to draw the air in from the returns and the fresh air intake and then draw it through filters and temperature treatment coils before discharging it back to the space served. They may be factory-built

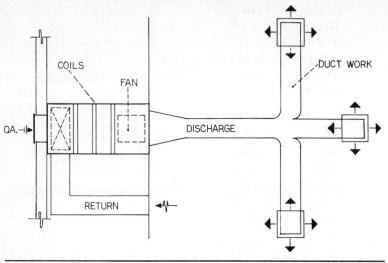

Figure 3   Air handler, plan view.

units in the smaller sizes or built-in-place units in the larger sizes and may be either high pressure or low pressure, in terms of static pressure generated in the discharge ductwork.

Blow-through units have the blower positioned between the filtering section and air treatment section, and actually blow the air across the temperature treatment coils instead of drawing it across. They are subdivided into single-zone and multizone units (see Figure 4), determined by whether the conditioned air leaves at the same temperature in one common duct or leaves the unit at different temperatures in different ducts under the control of separate space thermostats. The benefits of the multi-zone unit may be greater flexibility in terms of varying space temperature control, but in either single-zone or multi-zone units, the central station unit concept applies when the conditioning is done centrally and the air is distributed back to the spaces for heating or cooling.

Central station units may utilize hot water, steam, or electrical resistance coils for heating and chilled water or direct expansion refrigerant coils for cooling.

REMOTE CONDITIONING EQUIPMENT

In lieu of central equipment, it may be more desirable to provide space conditioning through the use of remote equipment located close to the space it serves and sized to handle just its respective area. Quite frequently, there is insufficient mechanical equipment space for central equipment, or occupational time periods are so staggered that the operation of a larger piece of central equipment is simply uneconomical for only a few select areas. In this case, remote equipment which can be operated independently of other units, may be more desirable, with its smaller energy requirements. Some of the more popular types of remote equipment follow.

Fan-Coil Units

So called because they contain a fan for moving air and a coil for heat exchange with the air, they can provide heating, cooling, or heating and cooling. A thermostat may start and stop the fan or control coil capacity, or both. Some units provide for the introduction of fixed, minimum amounts of fresh air during occupied periods, and any or all of the units may be tied to a time clock for shutdown during extended periods of unoccupancy. These units are well suited for corridors, small offices, bathrooms, and other areas where low-density occupancy coupled with varying thermal demands are present.

Unit Ventilators

Ideally suited to solving heating/cooling problems on an individual room basis when ventilation is also necessary, these units incorporate the fan and coil common to the fan-coil unit just discussed but in addition provide for ventilation through return air and fresh air dampers within the unit which can be controlled in sequence with the heating and cooling

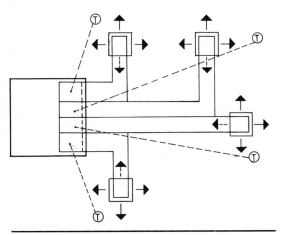

Figure 4   Multizone unit, plan view. Each thermostat controls its respective zone duct temperature.

coils. They may be heating only or heating and cooling, utilizing steam, hot water, or electricity for heat and chilled water for cooling. Their main feature is that they can take advantage of outside air for cooling when it is suitable, thereby saving energy that would otherwise be expended in generating mechanical cooling.

Unit ventilators, available in either horizontal or vertical configurations, find application wherever individual temperature modulation with attendant fresh air cooling is desirable. They are predominant in classrooms and lend themselves to a variety of control options, depending on whether just heating, or heating and summertime cooling are required, with or without night-time temperature setback in the winter.

The uniqueness of their being able to ventilate a space through the introduction of fresh air is recognized by the establishment of three basic cycles of control, which relate to how the introduction of outside air for ventilation is controlled. In cycle 1, 100 percent outdoor air is admitted at all times, except during warmup; In cycle 2, a minimum amount of outside air is introduced during the heating and ventilating stage, and up to 100 percent outside air is introduced during the ventilation cooling stage. And, in cycle 3, except during the warmup stage, outside air is varied by a mixed air controller to maintain a fixed temperature of air entering the unit's coil(s).

In a later chapter, in a subsection dealing with unit ventilators, on terminal unit control applications, you will recognize the employment of cycle 2 where, during the winter mode, fresh air for ventilation is introduced as described above.

Unit Heaters

Closely akin to the fan coil unit is the unit heater in that a coil and a fan are utilized, but the unit heater provides heating only. They are frequently hung from the ceiling for horizontal discharge service in storage areas, mechanical equipment rooms, or unfinished areas where their appearance is unobjectionable and rough-in for finishing the area is not required. Unit heaters are available also in floor-mounted models for vertical discharge, serving well in corridors or other areas where rough-in may be required. These are referred to as cabinet unit heaters. A "fan" switch may be provided on the "heating only" thermostat for the unit heater to permit the occupant to operate the fan for the circulation of air when hot water or other heating medium is not available.

Mixing Boxes

Taking advantage of a central fan system, mixing boxes are often employed as terminal units in the conditioned air distribution system, for final tempering of the air for specific point space conditioning. Both dual-duct and single-duct units are available. A dual-duct unit will be controlled by a thermostat and will select between warm or cool air being delivered to it through two separate duct systems from the central fan. A single-duct unit usually throttles down on the incoming cool air being delivered to it and thereafter adds heat via a heating coil on a fall in space temperature. This is known as a "variable volume box with reheat."

Reheat Coils

Another form of local tempering based on space demands is the pure reheat coil which also takes advantage of a central fan system and merely applies heat to the passing cool air as required by a space thermostat. Steam or hot water reheat coils may be used and a control valve will be modulated to maintain room conditions, or an electrical resistance heating coil can be used and controlled two-position, multistage two position, or modulated through an SCR, designed to vary the intensity of the sine wave for current reduction and temperature control. Pure reheat may be called for, too, at the end of a long conditioned air duct run, when in the winter an office at the end has trouble getting warm enough air to heat the space. Reheat permits the air temperature to be boosted enough to satisfy space demands.

Self-contained Incremental Units

Some heating/cooling situations may make extension of hot or chilled water lines and ductwork difficult to achieve. In those cases, all-electric self-contained heating/cooling units may be the answer. They are installed in the room where their work is to be done and are frequently finished off to appear as part of the cabinetry or room's adornments. Requiring electric power only, they lend themselves nicely to individualized service without piping or ducts. Electrical resistance heating may be used with an electric refrigeration compressor for cooling. The self-contained heat pump can also be utilized, with an electric resistance heat strip for supplemental heating only.

CENTRAL HEAT AND COLD GENERATING EQUIPMENT

Heating Boilers and Converters

Central generators of hot water or steam for heating serve the central fan and remote pieces of equipment. Oil-, gas-, or coal-fired or electric boilers may be chosen. Usually, each operates under control of its own operational and safety controls. Convertors are often employed in the case of steam boilers to exchange the heat in the steam to a hot water heating system. Condensate thus generated is returned to the boiler for regeneration into steam.

Hot water may be generated directly by a hot water boiler, with its own operational and safety controls. Hot water system temperatures are frequently maintained inversely with outdoor air temperature to assist in the maintenance of more even heating conditions, through the use of a three-way hot water control valve and a hot water sensor and an outdoor air temperature sensor, whose inputs to a controller are used to maintain hot water temperature through control valve modulation. The boiler bypass method, illustrated in Figure 5, sees a rising hot water discharge temperature as an indication of a drop in system demand, and this bypasses returning heating system water around the boiler, allowing discharge water temperature to fall back toward setpoint and the boiler to heat less water.

Water Chillers

For cooling the air being handled in the central fan and remote pieces of equipment, a chiller is usually employed, either reciprocating compression, centrifugal compression, or chemical absorption to generate chilled water in the neighborhood of 42° for delivery to the water-cooling coils within the air-handling units. Units are selected on the basis of tonnage from calculations concerned with the total heat load which the chiller will have to handle. Manufacturers generally provide controllers in the leav-

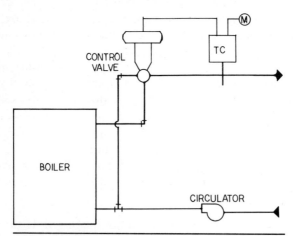

Figure 5   Boiler bypass.

ing chilled water to modulate machine capacity so as to maintain chilled water discharge temperature, and they provide low-limit thermostats to override discharge controllers so as to prevent freezeup.

For heat rejection from the condensers of the machines, cooling towers provide heat exchange to the atmosphere for the condenser water. Quite often their capacity is regulated by condenser water thermostats which may modulate condenser water flow to the tower and then start one or more cooling tower fans for forced air flow through the tower to increase the rate of heat exchange from the condenser water to the atmosphere.

Some condenser water systems provide for heat reclamation during intermediate weather when heat may be required in the perimeter areas of a building and cooling required within the core area of a building. Condenser water is routed through a heat exchanger which transfers the heat from the condenser water, which would otherwise be rejected to the atmosphere, to the heating hot water system, which may well be serving remote units on the perimeter of the building which are calling for heating. In this manner, economy is introduced into the heating/cooling system, because fuel is saved which would otherwise be required to raise the heating hot water system temperature for the benefit of those perimeter units which require heat. Automatic controls regulate the interface heat exchanger and position control valves for flow to the tower, if the interface heat exchanger cannot remove enough heat from the condenser water to prevent the condenser water temperature returning to the chillers from rising above a predetermined safety limit temperature.

Some mechanical cooling installations utilize air-cooled condensers, located outside, for their water chillers. The high-pressure gas is routed through finned coils outside, where a fan forces air circulation over the coils for removal of heat and condensation of the gas back to a liquid. A further refinement of this is the evaporative condenser, where the high-pressure refrigerant gas is routed to finned coils outside as before, except water is employed to aid in heat removal by being sprayed over the coils and evaporating on the surface of the coils, thereby removing greater amounts of heat, as heat from the gas within the coils is required to vaporize the water on the surface of the sprayed coils. Of course, as the heat is extracted from the refrigerant gas under pressure, condensation takes place, and the gas becomes a refrigerant liquid, ready to begin again the refrigerant cycle as it is pumped back to the evaporator of the chiller.

4 Motor Starters

MAGNETIC CONTACTORS PLUS
OVERLOAD PROTECTION

The mechanical equipment just discussed relies upon an electric motor for the motive force necessary for the propulsion of air through the air handlers or water through the piping systems. These electric motors, and the control and protection of them, deserve consideration, now, before we go into control applications, because controls invariably become involved with motor starters through the interlocks necessary to achieve the functions necessary for desired system operation.

Electric motors, one-half horse-power and smaller, usually will be single-phase 115V, and started manually or directly through an automatic device, such as a pressure switch or thermostat. Line currents are not so high that a magnetic starter with its control circuit is necessary, but a manual motor sentinel with motor running overcurrent protection is required and generally located close to the motor itself. Take the case of an above-ceiling exhaust fan drawing from rooms below and ducted to the outside. The motor protector could be mounted right at the fan motor itself, above the ceiling. Of course, it must be accessible, and usually is, through a lift-out ceiling or access door.

The motor protector is a horsepower-rated switch, incorporating thermal heaters which react to motor current, and which open the motor circuit should their setting be exceeded. It serves, too, as the local disconnect for anyone who may be required to service the fan or its motor later on.

Electric motors larger than one-half horsepower will usually be three-phase, utilizing the electrical characteristics of the building in which they are located, and usually the larger of the three-phase voltages available. Consider, for example, a building served 277/480V 3∅.

17

Three-phase 480V would be the voltage for which the building fan and pump motors would be selected. This voltage would be taken from three-phase 480V motor circuit distribution panelboards, while the 115V for lighting, receptacles, and fractional horsepower motors would be derived through transformers, sized and selected to feed 120/208-V 3∅ panelboards with branch circuit breakers. Much of the lighting, if it is fluorescent, could be installed as 277V, and the circuits could be taken out of the higher voltage panelboards. This is frequently the case. The 480-V 3∅ motors, then, will require motor starters, that can handle line-starting currents, motor running currents, and provide motor-running overcurrent protection. We will now consider such a motor starter.

The magnetic contactor with overload protection (Figure 6) is what a basic motor starter consists of, and many applications require no more than that. An air compressor, for example, would do quite well with such a basic starter, whose control circuit would probably be extended to a pressure switch, installed to sense tank pressure. A reset button, integral with the front of the starter, would be standard, so that the overload relay unit could be reset in the event its thermal elements reacted to motor overcurrent. When a starter drops out on overload, an inspection is called for, to determine the cause of the overload, before merely resetting the device.

Motor starters are horsepower and voltage rated, so reference to a manufacturer's catalog should enable a person to select a properly sized starter for a particular application. The horsepower to be controlled determines the size of the contacts in the starter itself, as well as the mass of its terminals and current carrying components. The voltage rating guarantees that its breakdown rating is well above the service voltage on which it will be used.

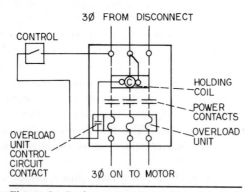

Figure 6   Basic motor starter. Magnetic contactor with motor running overcurrent protection unit.

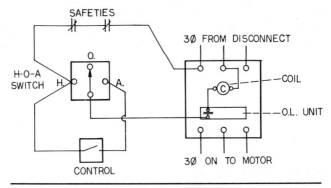

Figure 7 Starter and H-O-A switch.

Several different types of enclosures are available, and are given NEMA designations to give uniformity to the selection process. General duty enclosures are NEMA 1, while raintight enclosures are NEMA 3R. Other classifications denote dusttight, oiltight, and enclosures designed for hazardous locations. The environment in which the starter will be used determines the classification of enclosure to be selected.

Motors which will be operated by automatic devices generally will call for motor starters with cover-mounted, "hand-off-auto" selector switches. This manufacturer option permits automatic control through the "auto" leg of the selector switch and local manual operation through the "hand" leg of the selector switch. The "off" position provides for local shutdown of the piece of equipment.

Frequently, in automatic temperature control work, the "hand-off-auto" switch will be remoted to a local control panel, which may contain other automatic temperature control devices, as well. Looking at Figure 7, we see the contact of the automatic control device located so as to energize and deenergize the starter. The "hand" position merely parallels the "auto" contact. If this were a fan starter, safeties would be installed on the air handler and wired in series with the motor starter holding coil. In this manner, should any of the safeties sense a condition within their limits, they can open the control circuit and drop out the starter, thereby stopping the fan. Note that the safeties must be installed in the common control circuit, so that they may control fan operation when the selector switch is either in the "hand" or "auto" setting.

Motor starter control voltages are many times derived from control circuit transformers, installed inside the motor starter. Primary tappings of this transformer would be connected "line-side" of the starter. The secondary side of the transformer would have one side grounded and be properly fused, and the control circuit would be wired so that accidental grounding of the control circuit would not start the fan. For this reason, the contact control devices must be installed ahead of the holding coil, as the control circuit makes its way from the ungrounded side of the transformer to the grounded side. Accidental grounding of the circuit anywhere along the route will not, then, energize the starter. Were the situation reversed, as we see in Figure 8, accidental grounding would pick up the coil and energize the fan.

Remote control circuits are best derived from local distribution panelboards and should be properly labeled. One circuit may be extended to serve several motor starters, but in each case, a disconnect device must be provided adjacent to the local in-sight disconnect for the motor served, so that a shock hazard does not exist when just the motor disconnect is pulled. Such disconnects should deenergize the control circuit before it goes to any control or safety device. In this manner, all devices associated with the fan in question are "off" when the proper disconnects are pulled.

In 208-V 3∅ applications, a neutral may be pulled in with the three power conductors, to form a 120-V control circuit, which, of course, will be disconnected when the motor in-sight disconnect is pulled. This conductor must be an "identified" conductor, meaning white or grey insulation, which clearly denotes it as being a grounded conductor.

Motor starters will often have a coil which is the same voltage as the line-to-line voltage of the conductors serving the motor. In the case of a 480-V 3∅ motor, this would mean a 480-V coil, and there is no objection to this when the control circuit does not leave the motor starter enclosure. But when it is required to be extended to remote control or safety devices, good practice dictates that the control circuit be reduced in voltage and the starter coil changed to match the lower voltage for personnel protection and safety.

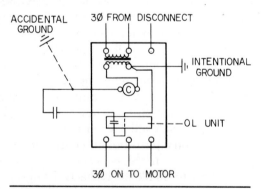

Figure 8 Incorrectly wired control circuit. Accidental ground after coil and before control energizes starter.

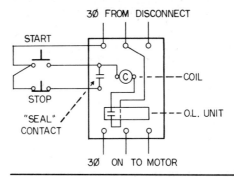

Figure 9 Momentary start-stop control. The start button is spring-loaded to return to "open" position after depressing. The "Stop" button spring-loaded to return to closed position.

When starting of equipment is to be accomplished manually, and it is not desirable to have the equipment start without personal intervention, a push-button with momentary contacts will be used. The special protection feature provided by this type of start-stop switch is "low voltage release," and when voltage is restored, the coil does not pick up until the start button is manually depressed again. Note in Figure 9 that the coil circuit is maintained by an auxilliary or "seal" contact, which is actuated by the armature, at the same time the main motor load contacts are actuated. The normally closed momentary stop button "secures" the holding circuit, and when depressed, opens the circuit to drop out the coil. If voltage is lost, the coil drops out, and the "seal" contact is opened, so that upon restoration of the voltage, the coil cannot pull in again until a person depresses the "start" button, which is normally open, and which momentarily parallels the "seal" contact to pull in the coil and reestablish the "seal" circuit. This type of motor control is ideal where automatic restarting without personnel observation is not desired.

In automatic temperature control work, the momentary push-button control circuit might be used on the initiating starter, or the starter which initiates startup of the cooling mode in a building. Quite often, manual startup of chilled water, condenser water pumps, and cooling tower fans is specified, and starting of the chilled water pump is selected as the first step. In this case, momentary push-button control might be called for, and the chiller, condenser water pump and cooling-tower fans would be started through interlock to auxilliary contacts, using the "auto" leg of their respective "hand-off-auto" selector switches. Note in Figure 10 how manual startup of the first pump brings on the rest of the associated equipment using auxilliary contacts within the starters. In this method,

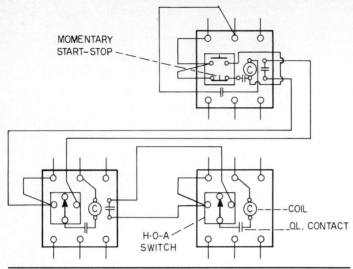

MOMENTARY
START–STOP

H-O-A
SWITCH

COIL

OL. CONTACT

Figure 10   Interlocked motor starters.

operation of the cooling equipment would not occur after a power failure, because the chilled water pump starter will release, the "seal" contact will open, and upon restoration of power, would not pick up again,
until someone manually depressed the start button. Many owners prefer
this, because they do not want their heavy equipment restarting without
supervision.

In another instance, automatic startup of all associated equipment
may be called for when a need for cooling occurs. Here, a "hand-off-
auto" selector switch would be used on the chilled water pump starter,
and an outdoor thermostat might be installed to start the chilled water
pump and associated equipment when the outdoor temperature rises to
perhaps 70°. In this manner, automatic restarting of cooling pumps and
chillers would occur after power failure, but appropriate time delays are
introduced into the control circuit to prevent short cycling of the chiller.
Restarting a chiller after shutdown for whatever reason without a minimum time interval introduces unnecessary stress on the chiller motor
and components and is in violation of most manufacturers' operational
procedures. Care must be taken in performing control wiring not to
circumvent manufacturer-installed time delays put there for the saftey of
the machine.

It is not uncommon to find in many applications the use of combination disconnects, that offer the fused disconnect and motor starter within
a common protective enclosure. These may be individual combination
units or units which are a part of a motor control center, where motor

control equipment is constructed into a large multisectioned, single-unit free-standing enclosure. Combination starters offer (1) motor circuit disconnect capabilities, (2) motor branch circuit overcurrent and short circuit protection, (3) motor control, and (4) motor running overcurrent protection, all within a common enclosure. Manufacturer options are available, too, which can add control-circuit transformers, selector switches, indicating lights, and extra auxilliary contacts. In automatic temperature control work, we become involved with starters and their accessories, when we connect our temperature control devices and other accessory equipment pertinent to the temperature control system.

5 Automatic Temperature Control Equipment

PNEUMATIC CONTROLS

Given a source of clean, dry compressed air at approximately 20 pounds, we have the "power" for a pneumatic system of automatic controls. To borrow a definition from Article 100 of the National Electrical Code, "automatic" means self-acting, operating by its own mechanism when actuated by some impersonal influence, as for example, a change in current strength, pressure, temperature, or mechanical configuration. To this, let us add "a change in relative humidity" as another type of change that affects automatic reaction.

Pneumatic sensors and controllers can be broadly defined as pressure regulators which react to temperature, relative humidity, or another pressure. A pneumatic thermostat, for example, mounted on the wall in a room, will vary its output in response to a change in room temperature. We can take advantage of this thermostat's reaction by piping its signal to a controlled device for corrective action. It is these regulators, then, that provide us with changing pneumatic signals that allow us to build a system that can measure, report, and react to changing environmental conditions within a building, and thereby bring about a change in the temperature of the air being delivered to the conditioned spaces. We will now examine the components of a pneumatic system.

THERMOSTATS

Perhaps the most evident part of a pneumatic temperature control system is the thermostat, because it inhabits the same areas as man, and represents the man-system interface. If man is uncomfortable, his first grievance is generally lodged against the most apparent feature of his

25

environmental system, the thermostat on his wall. His communication with it may take the form of "interested inspection," an examination to reveal to himself what the thermostat thinks the temperature is. Probably the thermostat will have a thermometer on its cover, indicating what the temperature is. Man then compares indicated temperature with thermostat setpoint, frequently visible and adjustable. Seeing that both agree, he may decide that he is either too warm or too cool and readjust the setpoint to suit himself. The thermostat will react, regulating its output to institute corrective action to bring space conditions to its new appointed control point, as desired by the room's occupant.

Thermostats are available as different types with varying features. Single-temperature thermostats work to maintain one setpoint, require one stable pressure for operation, and are either direct acting, increasing their output on a rise in temperature, or reverse acting, decreasing their output on a rise in temperature. Dual-temperature thermostats are indexed to one of two setpoints by a change in "main" pressure, as in the case of day-night thermostats which control at a lower setpoint at night in the winter and a higher setpoint during the day. Intentional indexing at a clock or manual station alternates the main pressure between two pressure settings to effect this switching of setpoints at the thermostat. Local override at the thermostat can be provided so occupants working beyond the night setback point may reindex their respective areas back to daytime setting for comfort while they work beyond normal hours. Submaster thermostats may be reset over a fixed span from a master signal responsive perhaps to outside air so as to lessen the deviation between inside and outside temperatures and to provide for some "swing" of inside temperatures as an energy-saving measure.

Summer-winter thermostats, designed to change their action (direct or reverse) in response to intentional indexing of main air pressures, permit the use of dual-temperature water coils in heating and air-conditioning units, where a 3-way valve, normally open to the water coil, will be modulated toward the coil bypass position on a rise in temperature in the winter when hot water is delivered to the unit and will be

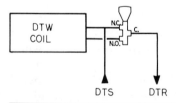

Figure 11 Three-way valve. Normally open to flow through dual-temperature coil.

modulated for greater flow through the coil on a rise in temperature in the summer when chilled water is being delivered to the unit.

Thermostats usually incorporate means to calibrate and change their throttling range. Calibration may be necessary from time to time and consists of adjusting the thermostat's temperature- sensing mechanism so that its response occurs at true temperature values, as relates to setpoint, and compensates for some shift which may have occurred owing to handling or excessive temperature extremes encountered during storage or handling before installation. Almost all manufacturers precalibrate at the factory, and recalibration in the field is usually not necessary. It is far more practical to install the thermostats and then return to calibrate them only if they demonstrate that they need it.

With increasing labor costs, there is a trend with some manufacturers toward thermostats, which are designed to be replaced rather than repaired. Resale pricing of such a unit is designed to encourage replacement rather than repair. Thermostats of this nature may remain an option, with the serviceable ones continuing to be available. Replaceable thermostats frequently are encapsulated during manufacturing, rendering the thermostat's internals inaccessible. Serviceable ones on the other hand can be disassembled for renewal of parts.

In addition to wall-mounted thermostats, unit-mounted thermostats are available where the presence of a wall-mounted one might not be desirable. Unit-mounted thermostats are installed usually under an access door on one side of the unit under control, and their sensing elements are located so as to sense the room-return air being induced to flow into the underside of the unit. Direct and reverse action models are available, as well as single-temperature, dual-temperature, and "summer-winter" models. The similarities between unit-mounted ones and wall-mounted ones are many. A basic difference is that wall-mounted thermostats sense temperature changes occuring at the thermostat itself, whereas unit-mounted models, with the thermostat itself mounted under an access door, have their sensing elements "remoted," to pick up room temperature, rather than temperatures under the access door within the unit. Also, wall-mounted thermostats offer adjustable setpoints graduated in degrees of temperature, as they are located at the "living level," at a height on the wall which samples room temperatures likely to be felt by occupants. Unit-mounted thermostats, on the other hand, with their sensing elements located close to the floor, will generally be fitted with adjustment dials marked "cooler-warmer," rather than degrees, because the temperature occurring at such a low level in the room does not represent temperatures experienced by people at the "living level."

Remote bulb thermostats are another type of thermostat used to sense air temperatures within ducts, water temperatures within piping, or even outdoor air temperatures, where the sensing bulb may be located under a protective sunshield in the outdoor air, or within the fresh air intake of an air handler. These devices, reacting to temperatures of the medium under control, rely upon capillary fill, expanding on a rise in temperature to impart motive force to the leverage mechanism of the thermostat to initiate changes in the pneumatic output of the device. Temperature range selections are usually quite broad, and these remote bulb thermostats will offer calibration and throttling range adjustment and direct or reverse action response. Submaster models may be offered, too, so that their setpoints can be varied from a master signal from either a manual or automatic device.

Airstream remote bulb thermostats should have averaging elements (see Figure 12), which traverse the cross-sectional area of the duct to ensure accurate sampling of duct air temperatures. Averaging elements can be available in lengths of up to 20 feet, with special capillary clips to facilitate "stringing" of the sensing element within the duct work.

Water temperature remote-bulb thermostats utilize separable socket thermal wells, which permit removal of the sensing bulb from the line without spillage of water from the system. These separable sockets are installed at the time the piping system is put together and permit the system to be "sealed" and filled before the thermostat sensing element is installed. Threaded fittings are installed in tees, in the heels of elbows, or sometimes in the side of large piping. Care should be taken, where possible, to angle the sensing bulb in the direction of flow. This prevents unnecessary flow stress being imparted to the separable socket well and aids in reducing system resistance and turbulence.

HUMIDISTATS

Relative humidity plays an important part in personal comfort. Humidistats react to relative humidity in the same way that thermostats react to temperature, modulating their output as relative conditions change. Often times, their signals are used in conjunction with signals from

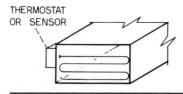

Figure 12 Averaging element–Strung across section of duct.

thermostats, to override thermal demands so as to start dehumidification, perhaps by energizing cooling. Thermostats thus overridden are usually designed into the system to bring on reheat as required to maintain space temperature, thereby lowering relative humidity.

Duct-mounted humidistats are located in the moving air and have no problem "sampling" the relative condition of the air. Wall humidistats, on the other hand, are sometimes at a disadvantage, unless means are provided to aspirate the device to ensure movement of air across the humidistat's sensing element for accurate sampling. For this reason, wall-mounted humidistats are best mounted in aspirating boxes, usually recessed in the wall, where control system air is used in the Venturi principle to induce room air to flow into the box, across the element, and follow the Venturi air stream out of the box into the room.

In industrial applications, the humidistat may be located in an aspirating cabinet, which employs a fan and filter to propigate the flow of clean, environmental air across the humidistat's element.

Three humidity-sensitive elements employed to react to relative humidity in humidistats are (1) wood, (2) hair, and (3) a hygroscopic celluose material. Each is connected to cause, within the humidistat, leverage movement, which is in turn imparted to the pneumatic pilot device to regulate device output.

SENSORS

Another pneumatic device in widespread use in commercial temperature control applications is the sensor-transmitter, which, like the thermostat, reacts to temperature, but which does it in a different way. The sensor-transmitter responds by changing its pneumatic output in a fixed relationship over a predetermined span, thereby providing a linear signal that increases in direct proportion to a temperature rise, in which each degree change can be related to specific change in pounds of pressure. This linearity allows us to calibrate receiver gauges in degrees temperature that match the temperature range of the sensor-transmitter, so we can readout the transmitted temperature in degrees although the signal being received is really pneumatic. The thermostat, on the other hand, modulates its output within its set throttling range. For example, consider a thermostat in a chilled-water line with a temperature range of 0 to 100°. The thermostat's setpoint might be 50°, with a throttling range of 10°. This means that no change takes place in thermostat output until the water temperature approaches 50°. At 45°, remembering a 10° throttling range, the thermostat's output begins to increase, until at 55°, the pneumatic output would be maximum. A continued rise above 55° could not cause a further rise in pneumatic output; it is already at maximum at 55°.

In the same application, a sensor-transmitter with a temperature range of 0 to 100° would begin at 0° to transmit a linear signal and would continue to do so until the temperature reached 100°, thereby providing us with a consistently graduated pneumatic signal over its entire range.

Many different fixed ranges for sensors are available. There is no throttling range adjustment. Usually, there is no calibration adjustment, as the factory does not recommend going into the transmitter for purposes of calibration. It is fixed and nonadjustable. There is no setpoint adjustment; its purpose is merely to transmit its linear signal over its fixed range. Another device, the receiver controller, to be discussed later, picks off a portion of the transmitted signal for control purposes.

Sensor-transmitters are available to transmit a pneumatic signal based on temperature, relative humidity, static pressure, and other pressures common to a commercial temperature control application.

CONTROLLERS

By their very name, controllers are devices which utilize transmitted information to monitor temperature deviations, compare them against setpoints, and take corrective action. This information may be a linear pneumatic signal, as we have discussed, or the motive force of gas fill in a capillary and bulb system. Controllers differ from thermostats in that they are usually larger-case instruments, offer more in terms of adjustments or indication, and are frequently mounted in control panels.

Considering the self-contained controller, we find that it features (1) a sensing element with gas fill; (2) a setpoint selector; (3) a throttling range or proportional band adjustment; (4) frequently, direct or reverse action adjustment; (5) may incorporate manual, remote-reset capabilities; (6) can offer a deviation-reset feature, which automatically shifts setpoint to compensate for drift in controlled point; (7) very often includes an automatic, remote-reset feature , in which a second sensor signal is piped into the instrument to automatically shift setpoint inversely with second temperature deviation; and (8) provides a gauge manifold for multiple pressure indications. Not all of the above features will of necessity be present in any given controller, and the line of differentiation between a remote-bulb thermostat and a controller, temperature controller, is not that definite. Frequently, the more simple self-contained controllers are referred to as thermostats, and the remote-bulb thermostats are frequently referred to as temperature controllers.

The receiver controller makes use of a pneumatic signal from another instrument. It reacts to pressure, whether it be from a temperature transmitter, pressure transmitter, or relative-humidity transmitter. Its setpoint may be made in degrees, but only if a temperature scale is installed which matches the range of the temperature transmitter to which it is connected.

Receiver controllers know only pressure, and settings made on the device are really pressure settings. The input ports will generally have threaded taps into which a gauge can be inserted. Since the inputs are linear with respect to temperature change, gauges calibrated in degrees that match the transmitter are easily utilized to read at the receiver controller what the temperature is at the sensor-transmitter. This assists greatly in calibration.

Receiver controllers lend themselves very well to centralized panel mounting, in which multiple instruments can be grouped together, receiving signals from variously located remote sensors. This creates a central temperature adjustment point and, with the panel or cabinet locked, gives a certain degree of security to access to the controllers and their setpoints.

Setpoint, proportional band adjustments, and calibration capabilities are, of course, part of the receiver controller, but there is also an authority adjustment which determines to what extent the resetting signal will affect setpoint. There is a formula which the manufacturer provides that is used in selecting the authority adjustment.

Many of the receiver controllers can be made to two-position at a certain setpoint, making them ideal for use in changeover systems, where sudden indexing is desired at any given point. Field-changing from direct to reverse action or vice versa is available in some but not all receiver controllers.

RELAYS

To accomplish the various control sequences that might be called for on any given job, pneumatic relays of varying types are provided.

High-pressure, Low-pressure Selector Relay

Given two or more pneumatic signals, it may be desirable to select the lowest or the highest, or both, for control purposes. In this case, pneumatic relays that can select and pass on the lowest-highest signal are necessary. In Figure 13, we see a selector relay which can be used to transmit the lowest input, the highest input, or both. This particular type of selector relay can take multiple inputs and discriminate between the

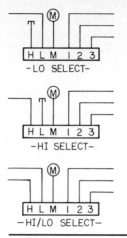

Figure 13 High or low pressure selector relay.

lowest and the highest. If these signals were from thermostats that are direct acting, the highest signal would be from the warmest thermostat and could be used to bring on cooling or to reset a cold deck temperature in a multizone unit. The lowest signal would be from the coolest thermostat and could be used to bring on heating or to reset a hot deck temperature in a multizone unit.

Diverting or Switching Relay

In pneumatic temperature control work, requirements routinely occur where diverting or switching of pneumatic signals is required to affect a given sequence of operations. This calls for the switching relay which reacts to an indexing signal to change connections between ports, as illustrated in Figure 14.

Notice that this relay is double-pole, double-throw, terms analagous to an electric relay. Without an indexing signal, both sections of the relay

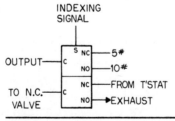

Figure 14 DPDT pneumatic switching relay.

have their common ports connected to their respective normally open ports. The top section is providing 10-lb output to some device, and the lower section has exhausted air from a normally closed valve, so that the valve is shut. The thermostat signal at the normally closed port cannot reach the valve.

When an indexing signal is applied, the relay "switches over," and connects the respective common ports with their normally closed ports. Now the top section is delivering 5-lb air, and the lower section has placed the thermostat in control of the normally closed valve.

Frequently, the switchover setpoint is adjustable, so that a modulated signal from a sensor or controller can be applied to the indexing port, labeled "S" for signal.

Reversing Relay

The ability to create a pneumatic signal proportionate and inverse to another is a necessary feature of a pneumatic control system. For this reason there is the reversing relay. In a packaged air handler which uses electric strip heaters and a direct expansion refrigeration coil, it is desirable to have both heating and cooling "fail safe" to the "off" position, in the event air pressure for the control system is lost for any reason. This would require normally open pressure-actuated, electric control switches or relays for both the heating and cooling control application. Notice in Figure 15 that a thermostat with a direct-acting signal is used to control both heating and cooling. The signal can be piped directly to the cooling pressure switch, because it is normally open, and on a rise in temperature, we want to close the contact. But the heating pressure switch uses a normally open contact, also, so that loss of air deenergizes heat. An increasing signal from a direct-acting thermostat which is too warm would close the normally open contact in the heating switch. Therefore,

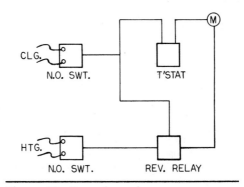

Figure 15   Reversing relay.

the signal must be reversed. The reversing relay is installed between the thermostat and the heating switch and changes the incoming direct signal to a reverse one, using a separate air feed from perhaps the same main that feeds the thermostat. The reversing relay is a pilot-operated device, so the signal from the thermostat is used to regulate the reversing relay's output in an inverse manner. Fail-safe protection is still provided, because removal of the main air source will cause a collapse of output signals, and the normally open pressure switches will break their respective electrical circuits.

Reversing relays generally track proportionately in an inverse manner to the input signal, but some manufacturers offer a biasing feature which allows you to shift the start point, so that signal response to input is delayed, when it might be desirable to prolong relay output in order to achieve proper sequencing. Consider an application where NC (normally closed) steam valves with the same spring range are to be sequenced from a direct-acting thermostat. In Figure 16, a pressure switch is added, too, to stop a circulator serving the steam to a hot water heater, and it has a normally closed contact. A rise in hot water temperature causes an increase in thermostat signal output. Valve 1 (V-1) is operated through a reverse linear relay, and modulates 13–8lb to close as the thermostat signal increases from 3–10lb. V-2 is operated through a reverse bias relay, and modulates 13–8lb to close as the thermostat signal increases from 9–15lb. The pressure switch controlling the circulator might be set to open its normally closed contact at 15lb, or when both valves were closed. Figure 17 indicates the relationship between the thermostat's output and the output from both reversing relays. In Figure 17, the reverse linear relay is labeled R-1, and the reverse bias relay is labeled R-2.

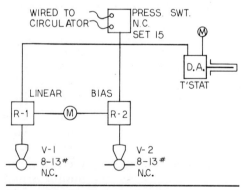

Figure 16   Reversing relays.

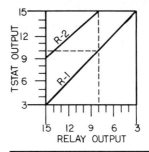

Figure 17 Linear and bias reversing relay outputs.

The bias reversing relay would probably have an adjustable starting point, and here we have adjusted it to start at 9 pounds.

Averaging Relay

Signals from thermostats or sensors are sometimes used for reset purposes, where the thermostat or sensor dictates to another device what corrective action to take. It may be desirable, in the case of several thermostats, to average their signals, particularly if the device being "piloted" is in turn regulating the temperature of the air or water being delivered to the spaces in which all the thermostats are located.

In the case of duct temperatures, if four thermostats are controlling their individual reheat coils, and at the same time resetting a duct temperature controller, an averaging relay could be used to average the demand for reset. In so doing, no one thermostat would be given complete control of resetting the duct temperature. In some cases, this could unbalance conditions in areas served by the other thermostats. The averaging relay averages the need for reset and applies this averaged signal to the duct temperature controller. Most likely this averaged signal would be used to lower duct temperatures over a predetermined reset range, assuming direct-acting thermostats. Such a range might lower duct temperature from 65° with no reset to 55° with full reset. Thus, the averaging relay (see Figure 18), receiving four separate signals from individual thermostats, is able to prevent any one signal from taking complete control of the controller's reset range, and in so doing, ensures more moderate changes more in keeping with total need.

When the total number of inputs exceeds the capacity of any one relay, they can be cascaded, when the output of one relay inputs to another along with remaining signals to be averaged.

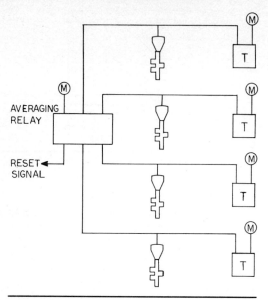

Figure 18 Averaging relay averaging signals from four thermostats.

Booster Relay

When long distances are to be covered by pneumatic signal or control lines, a booster relay may be employed to renew the intensity of the signal and overcome drop in line pressure encountered in long spans. Plainly and simply, a booster or capacity relay amplifies on a 1 to 1 ratio the signal it receives, using a separate main air source. Its output is purely proportional to its input. In Figure 19, we see the input piped to port S and a fresh air supply piped to port M. Output, or branch, comes from port B. Manufacturers' designations may differ, although the function is the same.

Some booster relays may also double as a low-pressure selector be-

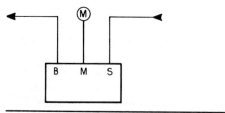

Figure 19 1 : 1 booster relay.

cause the output is linear with the input when main is constant, and it follows the lower input signal. Conversely, if main drops below input, output tracks the diminishing main, because the device is a pilot-operated unit, and no more pressure can be transmitted than there is available in main.

Booster relays can be found in use quite often where a low-capacity controller is operating a large-volume actuator, and the capacity required to stroke the actuator as fast as may be required is not available from the controller itself. So a booster relay with a larger capacity is installed between the two to increase the rate of response.

Sequencing Relay

In an earlier part of this chapter, we touched on biasing capabilities in the reversing relay. A parallel-action relay that offers biasing is the sequencing relay. "Parallel-action" refers to the fact that its action, direct or reverse, parallels its input: it does not reverse, but merely responds in like manner and sends on a direct signal for a direct input. But it may be adjusted (some models may be fixed, not adjustable) so that its output begins at a later point than its input. Its output is said to be sequenced, so that actuators with similar spring ranges, one connected to the sequencing relay's output and the other connected to the same line with the relay's input, can be modulated on a "first one, then the other" basis. In Figure 20, note that one valve (V-1) is piped directly to the thermostat output, and the other (V-2) is piped to the output of the sequencing relay. Although both have the same spring range, one will actuate before the other. Therefore, a sequencing of the two valves is obtained, even though both are identical in terms of their response range (spring range).

The sequencing relay gives us flexibility in our ability to create special modulation where one action must follow another in a one-two manner.

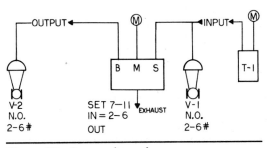

Figure 20 Sequencing relay.

Minimum Position Relay

Most economizer cycles on air handlers make use of the minimum position relay, which establishes a minimum output of an actuator or other controlled device, anytime the unit is in operation. But a very important feature of the minimum position relay is that it can be overridden by a larger signal coming to its pilot port.

The minimum position relay is adjustable, so that various minimum settings are available. Some manufacturers make the device in a switch configuration, with a knob that facilitates ready adjustment. That way, if the device is mounted on a panel front, the switch's dial positions can be labeled, so the operator knows where he is setting the minimum. With the relay model, the adjustment is perhaps less accessible, which sometimes is an advantage if ready access is not desirable. Of course, the relay or switch could always be mounted inside the panel, thereby limiting adjustments to authorized personnel.

A gauge is best used in conjunction with the minimum position relay, so that its output can be observed. When the spring range of the actuator is known, positioning becomes a simple matter of interpolation, based on the percentage of the actuator's spring range to which the actuator diaphragm is pressurized. With a 5- to 10-lb spring, a setting of 6lb should produce a minimum position setting of the actuator at 20 percent of stroke.

Hesitation Relay

It may become necessary in control work to introduce a pause into controlled device regulation, to create a deadband in terms of response, for purposes of blending the action of one device into another. Here the hesitation relay would be used, because its output may be adjusted so that it begins its response, pauses perhaps midway through, and then picks it up again to continue toward completion of its reaction. In Figure 21, notice that damper motor M-1 has a spring range of 3 to 13lb, whereas damper motor M-2's spring has a range of 5 to 10lb. M-1 is used on the fresh air damper of a small unit, and M-2 is used on the face and bypass damper of the same unit. M-2, without air, positions its damper so that it is open fully to the heating coil and closed fully to bypass, so all of the air passing through the unit is now heated. On a rise in temperature at thermostat T-1, it begins to increase its output (direct acting) to both M-1 and M-2, but hesitation relay R-1 is installed between T-1 and M-1 to introduce hesitation when the damper controlled by M-1 is partially open so that M-2 may, in the meantime, close off air flow through the heating coil and bypass it around the heating coil, because M-1 will now begin to fully open its damper to fresh air for cooling in order to satisfy T-1.

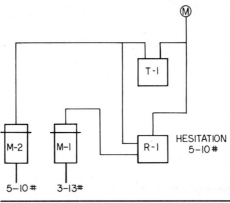

Figure 21   Hesitation relay.

The graphic picture of R-1's reaction to T-1's output, Figure 22, illustrates the response R-1 makes to T-1 and the resultant signal from R-1 onto damper motor M-1. Notice that no further increase in output from R-1 occurs from the time T-1's output reaches 5lb until it reaches 10lb. It is during this deadband that M-2 (see Figure 21) will respond and bypass the air flowing through the unit around the heating coil, because no further heating is now desired. In effect, we have a warm-up cycle of control, since the normal equilibrium point of T-1 is between 8 and 10lb, and at that point M-1 (see Figure 21) will be admitting minimum fresh air, while M-2 modulates to maintain space temperatures. When the space is cold as sensed by T-1, all fresh air is temporarily closed off, until space temperatures come within range of T-1's sensitivity adjustment. This long-established warmup cycle finds use quite often in unit ventilators serving classrooms or other activity areas. At the opposite end of the cycle, we have a ventilation cycle which can make use of fresh air,

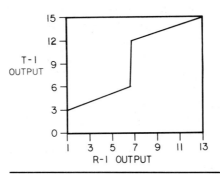

Figure   22   Hesitation   relay   response graphic.

when suitable, for cooling of spaces, with all air being bypassed around the heating coil.

Sometimes the sequence is accomplished through the use of an actuator with a split-range spring, but where necessary, the hesitation relay is ready to serve.

Pneumatic-Electric Relay

Control of electrical equipment by pneumatic controls calls for an interface control which can make and break an electrical circuit in response to a pneumatic signal. A set or sets of contacts operated by mechanical motion from a diaphragm or bellows is closed and opened to start or stop mechanical equipment employing electric motors by a pneumatic-electric relay, popularly called a PE. If we set the contacts to make on a pressure rise at 10.2lb, and pipe the PE to a 0 to 100° fresh air temperature transmitter, we could energize mechanical cooling on a rising outdoor air temperature at 60°. If the PE had a 1/2lb differential, a falling outdoor air temperature would open the contact at 9.7lb or 56°. So we see that the PE allows us to utilize our pneumatic signal to control electrical circuits.

PEs find *wide* use in pneumatic temperature control systems. Fans are started and stopped, electric heat is energized and deenergized, and mechanical cooling is switched on and off, all in response to pneumatic signals from pneumatic controls in charge of the environmental requirements. Although the PE is a pneumatic instrument, it is also an electrical instrument, and it must be properly applied within its voltage and current ratings and wired in accordance with applicable codes. The instrument mechanic will mount and pipe the PE, and the electrician will wire it.

The most frequently encountered electrical switch configuration in PEs is the single-pole double-throw (SPDT) switch, which lends itself to being wired either normally open or normally closed. This refers to the condition of the electrical circuit through the PE in the absence of any signal whatsoever. A normally closed PE would open the circuit on a pressure rise, and a normally open PE would close the circuit on a pressure rise. PEs controlling electric heat are generally wired normally open, so that if air pressure is lost for any reason, the electric heat will fail-safe to the "off" position. Conversely, a PE wired to alarm in the event air pressure is lost for any reason would be wired normally closed, and its contact would close an electrical circuit on loss of signal to annunciate pneumatic shutdown.

All three terminals of an SPDT PE may be wired, if it is desirable to utilize a common feed and energize a leg on pressure rise or drop. A two-position pneumatic signal might be used to open or close a damper, and a PE piped to receive the same signal may at the same time be required to energize a green pilot light for open and a red pilot light for closed. If the damper is normally closed, the normally open contact of the PE would be wired to the green light, and the normally-closed contact of the PE would be wired to the red light.

Electric-Pneumatic Relay

When necessary to obtain pneumatic response from an electrical signal, an electric-pneumatic relay is used, popularly called an EP. The EP is actually a solenoid air valve and is *widely* used in pneumatic temperature control work for interlocking pneumatic functions with electrical signals. Temperature controls for an air-handling unit are usually prohibited from operation unless the unit is in operation itself. By wiring the EP to the load side of a fan starter, we can energize and deenergize our pneumatic control system in unison with fan startup and shutdown. In Figure 23, we see the EP connected on the load side of the starter and wired L-1 and L-2 so that when the voltage is released to the motor through the motor controller our EP is energized at the same time. In this instance, the voltage of the EP must match the voltage utilized to run the motor. Another option in connections would be to wire the EP in parallel with the motor starter holding coil and through an auxilliary contact. This would allow us to match our EP voltage with the control circuit instead of the motor. The auxilliary contact would indicate that the starter had "pulled in."

EPs used in control work are three-ported, with one common, one normally open, and one normally closed. These denotations refer to the passage through the port when the EP is at rest, or deenergized. Most often, the air fed to the controls is piped to the common port, main air is piped to the normally closed port, and the normally open port is open to exhaust (atmosphere). When energized, the normally open port is

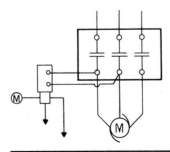

Figure 23   EP wired to load-side of starter.

blocked, and common is connected to the normally closed port, allowing main air to be fed onto the controls. The control system is put into operation simultaneous with fan operation.

Suppose it was required that a common pneumatic signal was needed whenever either of two fans started. It might be that either of the fans is to be operated independently of the other, yet they share a common fresh air intake. In this case, we would need to open a fresh air damper anytime either or both of the fans were in operation. Here we would pipe two EPs in parallel. We see in Figure 24 that either of the EPs can open the fresh air damper, and if both are energized, it will open, too. The parallel piping arrangement permits air to flow to the fresh air damper actuator so it can serve either fan.

EPs, used in conjunction with PEs, can effectively minimize control-wiring requirements in a pneumatic temperature control system. Consider an exhaust fan which is required to be interlocked with a supply fan so that when the supply fan starts, the exhaust fan will start also. The starters for these fans may be 100 feet apart. This would necessitate control wiring between the two so that the holding coil circuit of the exhaust fan can be wired through an auxilliary contact of the supply fan starter. To minimize the wire requirements, we could install our EP at the supply fan starter and wire it to energize with the supply fan starter. Then, with main air piped to the normally closed port, we would pipe the common port to a PE 100 feet away at the starter for the exhaust fan, and the PE would be wired into the start circuit of the exhaust fan starter. Thus the pneumatic signal would accomplish our interlock for us, and wiring requirements would be reduced to local connections and some greenfield instead of 100 feet of conduit and two wires.

Many interlocking situations arise in temperature control work, and the EP is our electrical-to-pneumatic interface that allows us to index pneumatic actuation from electrical impulses. In engineering temperature control work, consideration needs to be given to choices relating to the economies between doing it electrically or pneumatically.

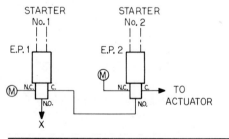

Figure 24   Parallel piped EPs.

ACTUATORS

The pneumatic temperature control system is designed to regulate and maintain temperatures, and when this is accomplished through modulation of steam, water, or air flow, actuators are employed to operate control valves or dampers. Diaphragm actuators are by far the most common. For control valves, they usually take the form of round wafer-type diaphragms frequently manufactured from rubber or rubber derivatives and attached within the diaphragm housing so that air pressure building up on one side can move the diaphragm in the opposite direction and impart motive force to the valve stem so as to "stroke" the valve stem to regulate flow through the valve. Different sizes of actuators are available, larger ones for larger valves, where greater force may be required to overcome steam or water system pressures which would tend to work against an actuator trying to close a valve against system pressures.

Damper actuators are most often of the piston type with rolling diaphragms, allowing the piston to move back and forth within a cylinder in response to pneumatic pressures. Here, too, actuators are available in different sizes to deal with various torque requirements. Damper actuators generally stroke out to move a crankarm attached to a damper drive shaft, or they may be mounted so as to reposition a drive blade, which in turn moves the other blades of the damper which are linked to it.

Both control valve and damper actuators generally have a built-in spring which opposes the pneumatic pressure, and which is overcome by the pneumatic signal in order to operate the actuator and operate the valve or damper. In this manner, the actuator is "spring-returned" to its normal position when the pneumatic signal is removed, allowing us to design for normally open or normally closed control valves and dampers. Different spring ranges are offered, so that we may sequence the action of one with the action of another, when a one-two action is called for, and when we don't want to use sequencing relays. The selection of spring ranges also affects the close-off capacity of the actuator, because when a control signal is applied in excess of that required to just overcome the spring range, we have greater close-off potential than when a signal is applied to an actuator whose spring has a range, the top of which peaks at the same time as our pneumatic signal.

Consider a 3- to 15-lb pneumatic signal from a pneumatic controller. For an actuator whose spring range is 2 to 7lb, our signal is more than sufficient, and the overlapping signal from 8 to 15lb acts on top of the 2 to 7lb actually required and ensures solid, positive positioning of the actuator. But an actuator whose spring range is 8 to 13lb, does not move until the signal reaches 8lb and is not in as good a position to effect close-off against high system pressures as an actuator whose range is 2 to 7lb and can take advantage of the remaining 8 to 15lb from the controller to make sure it holds shut as required. Therefore, torque requirements play an important part in selection.

So selection of our actuators must be governed by the following considerations:

1. Torque requirements
2. Sequencing requirements
3. Close off requirements

Also to be considered in some situations are mounting arrangements, when different brackets are offered, and direct or reverse action, when these options are available.

DAMPERS

Regulation of air flow in heating, ventilating, and air-conditioning systems is accomplished by automatic control dampers. Two basic modes of damper control prevail: two-position and modulating. Fresh air dampers which are sized specifically for minimum fresh air requirements in a predominantly return air system would be two-positioned opened or closed by an EP. So our system would be open to fresh air only when the fan was running. Larger fresh air dampers, working in conjunction with return air and perhaps relief-air dampers, would be modulated from perhaps a minimum position to all the way open, when conditions were right.

Two basic styles of damper construction are prevalent: parallel-blade dampers and opposed-blade dampers. Simpler, less expensive parallel-bladed dampers are used for two-position service, and the somewhat more expensive opposed blade dampers are used for modulated control of air flow. In the simplified Figure 25, we see the opposed blade damper with blades linked so that each blade travels in a direction opposite from the one immediately next to it. This permits better regulation of air flow

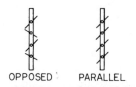

OPPOSED   PARALLEL

Figure 25   Damper blade arrangement.

and provides us with flow curves more linear in nature, so that a percentage movement of the damper actuator yields roughly the same percentage air flow change across the damper. Manufacturers offer charted flow curves to show evidence of damper performance, and these are good tools to be used in the selection of dampers for control purposes.

Frequently (and ever more so with the emphasis on energy conservation) tight closeoff is essential, and manufacturers rate their dampers in terms of percentage of leakage at stated approach velocities. Blade edging and end seals are available to help ensure minimum leakage when the actuator has the damper closed off. Oil-impregnated bronze bearings are regularly used to prevent the necessity of routine oiling of blade bearings.

The parallel blade damper has blades that travel in the same direction. Over-lapping edges of the blades come together in shutter-fashion. Close-off is maintained until the damper opens again, and the blades rotate 90° to lie in a horizontal, full-open position.

VALVES

Steam, hot water, and chilled water are the flowing temperature transfer media requiring regulation for temperature control by control valves, which can modulate coil capacity by throttling flow. Pneumatic temperature control valves predominantly are of the diaphragm-actuated type, utilizing varying control signal for positioning of the valve in response to temperature demands. Control valves 2 in and smaller historically feature threaded, or screwed, pipe connections, while valves 2 1/2 in and larger are flanged, requiring bolts, nuts, and gaskets. But pipeline size alone is not the basis for the sizing selection process. Manufacturers rate their control valves in terms of flow capacity, allowing for the internal porting of the valve. This rating figure is known as the coefficient of flow and is equal to the number of gallons of 60° water that will flow through a valve in one minute with a pressure drop of one pound. This number is called C_v. It is calculated for a specific application through the use of the following formulas. It is a necessary step in the selection of a control valve, because oversizing robs the valve of its ability to effectively modulate and introduces "hunting," and undersizing prevents full flow necessary when full-load conditions exist. Let us give some consideration, now, to development of the required C_v.

Steam C_v Selection

Designers of heating, ventilating, and air-conditioning systems will usually state steam coil capacities on job drawings or in job specifications.

The temperature control technician must select his steam valve to serve a designated steam coil by finding the C_v required and then choosing the correct valve to match it, based on the valves published C_v.

$$C_v = \frac{\text{lb/hr} \times \sqrt{V}}{63.5 \times \sqrt{PD}}$$

where lb/hr = pounds per hour of steam which our valve must pass when fully open

V = specific volume of steam at the given inlet pressure (from a steam chart)

63.5 = a constant

PD = allowable pressure drop which we can take through the valve

For this example, let's assume a requirement of 500lb/hr of 10-lb steam and an allowable pressure drop of 5lb. The HVAC designer has based his steam heating coil capacity requirements on 5lb of steam in the coil, so with a 10lb supply, we are allowed a 5lb drop. (Drop should be limited to a maximum of 50 percent). We enter 500 on the top line of our formula, and multiply it by 4.061, which we find in our steam table as the square root of the specific volume of 10-lb steam. On the bottom line, we enter our constant, 63.5, and multiply it by the square root of 5, which is 2.236. With our values inserted, our formula looks like this.

$$C_v = \frac{500 \times 4.061}{63.5 \times 2.236}$$

This yields a numerator of 2,031 and a denominator of 142, or an answer of 14.3. The C_v of our valve should be at least as large as 14.3. Where this would fall in between two given C_v, the next larger one would be selected.

Water C_v Selection

The process is similar for water valves, but a different formula is used, and is somewhat simpler.

$$C_v = \frac{\text{GPM}}{\sqrt{PD}}$$

where GPM = gallons per minute of water which our valve must pass when fully open

PD = allowable pressure drop which we can take through the valve

Here again, water coil capacities will usually be stated by the HVAC designer, so we may have it for development of our control valve size. For control valves on water service, a 2-lb drop is usually taken as the standard allowable, unless stated otherwise in the job specifications.

For this example, let us assume a requirement of 50 gallons per minute. Fifty becomes our numerator, and the square root of 2, which is 1.41, becomes our denominator. With these values inserted, our formula looks like this.

$$C_v = \frac{50}{1.41}$$

Our answer here is 35, so our selection of a control valve for this water service application calls for a C_v of at least 35, or where this falls in between two given C_v, the next size larger would be used.

So this, then, the development of valve size, becomes the first step in our selection process, as we endeavor to choose the best valve, best suited for the application at hand.

Valve Design

Two-way or straight-through control valves are generally used on steam service, and on water service where provisions are made for regulation of head pressures. The straight-through control valve dead ends the flow coming to it whenever the valve closes. Single-seated valves offer good closeoff, unless head pressures are quite high and there is concern about the valve and its actuator overcoming upstream pressure. In this instance, a double-seated valve may represent the best application, since it tends to be self-balancing. Upon examination of Figure 26, we see the plug working against flow as closeoff occurs in the single-seated valve, whereas in the double-seated valve, as one plug moves against the flow, the other (on the same stem) modulates *with* flow to restrict let-through and tends to balance the effect of head pressure, since it would tend to be

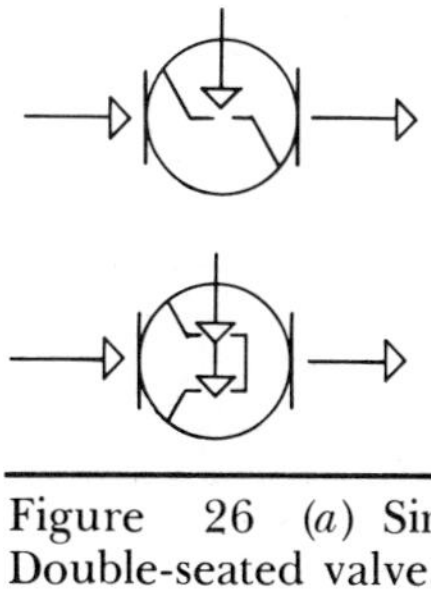

Figure 26 (*a*) Single-seated valve. (*b*) Double-seated valve.

"pulled" into the port. This usually permits the use of a somewhat smaller actuator than a single-seated valve of the same size. The vast majority of temperature control valve applications permit the use of single-seated control valves, since most manufacturers offer a selection of topworks or actuators for modulation of the valve.

In terms of downward stem movement, a control valve body can be classified as "normally open" or "normally closed". Valves featuring plugs that move toward closed on a downward movement of the valve stem are normally open, whereas valves whose plugs move toward open on a downward movement of the valve stem are normally closed. This is derived from the fact that most temperature control valves employ direct-acting actuators that react to drive the valve stem downward on an increase in control signal to the actuator. Notice in Figure 27 that the normally open valve body plug is situated over the ported opening, but the normally closed valve body plug is situated under the ported opening of the valve. A direct acting topworks will apply downward movement to close the normally open valve, but the same downward pressure on the normally closed valve will open it. This direct-acting topworks would be spring-loaded to lift the stem in the absence of pneumatic signal. Hence the normally open valve would be open and the normally closed valve would be closed. This consideration comes into play as we decide how our application should "fail-safe". Heating valves are generally applied to "fail-safe" to the open position (normally open valves), should control air be lost, so that the building would not freeze in the winter. Cooling valves usually "fail-safe" to the closed position (normally closed valves) so that the building will not overcool in the summer. Also, by adhering to this practice, we are able to sequence heat and cooling with the same direct-acting signal from a controller or thermostat.

Since actuators or topworks for valves are available for either direct-acting or reverse-acting applications, we are able to reverse the action of any valve we might have through the use of the proper actuator. Consider a normally open valve body which needs to be normally closed in

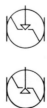

Figure 27 (*a*) Normally open valve. (*b*) Normally closed valve.

any given application, in order to achieve redesign. A reverse-acting actuator, which is spring-loaded to hold the stem down without pneumatic signal, would open the valve by lifting the stem and would make our valve reverse acting, or normally closed. Versatility of this type in a manufacturer's line of temperature control valves is a valuable feature to the temperature control designer, as he plans for the best action of a valve for any given application.

Three-Way Valves

Modulating control of water flow, both hot and chilled water, is most often accomplished through the use of three-way control valves. These valves offer the advantage of maintaining constant flow in the hot- or chilled-water piping system while at the same time regulating flow of water through the coil. When three-way valves are used, other provisions for regulation of head pressure are not required since three-ways do not dead-end the flow at the coil under control.

The three-way valve is so called because there are three openings into which or from which water flows. Single-seated, three-way valves are the type predominantly employed in temperature control work, and they are installed so that they are operated in a mixing or self-balancing application. Double-seated, three-way valves are required when the valve is to be installed in a diverting application. As Figure 28 shows, the mixing valve has water coming into two openings and flowing from one,

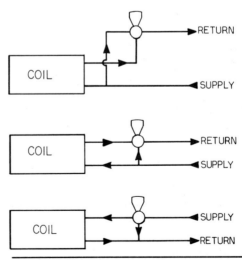

Figure 28 Three-way valves. (*a* and *b*) Mixing application. (*c*) Diverting application.

Figure 29 (*a*) Three-way mixing valve. Equal pressure on both sides of the plug helps balance torque requirements. (*b*) Three-way diverting valve. Equal pressure on each of the two plugs helps balance torque requirements.

whereas the diverting valve has water coming into one opening and flowing from two. Because of the equalizing effect of head pressure into two openings of the valve in the mixing application, a single, double-sided plug can be used (see Figure 29), and operated to work between first one ported opening and then the other, to blend the incoming waters for regulation of flow through the coil. On the other hand, the diverting valve, which has to "divert" a common flow into one of two directions, would tend to be slammed in one direction or the other, if it were not for the double plug which takes advantage of the incoming water pressure to balance itself by virtue of the manner in which the water flows past the plug, in much the same manner as the double-seated, straight-through valve is balanced. Single-seated, three-way valves used on diverting service generally cause difficulties because of excessive chattering owing to the plug being slammed shut as it approaches the seat. Single-seated, three-ways should be used for mixing applications only, except, in some instances, in cases of small flows and low pressure applications, with sufficiently large actuators.

Depending on the actuator selected, three-way valves can be piped normally open or normally closed to flow through the coil. In this manner, the three-way valves, like their straight-through cousins, can be applied in different "fail-safe" applications, so that they assume a desired position in the event of loss of signal, and so that sequencing can be accomplished in air-handling units with separate chilled and hot water coils.

AIR COMPRESSORS

Of course, the heart of our pneumatic system is the air compressor, carefully chosen to ensure that its size is sufficiently adequate to serve our pneumatic temperature control system and any future additions that may be in the plans for the future.

Compressors are selected by totaling the air consumption of the *air-consuming* devices in our system to arrive at the number of cubic feet per minute (CFM) they will demand. Not all of our devices use air. Diaphragm actuators are dead-ended, that is, they receive air from a controller and respond to it, but that same air must be exhausted by the controller to allow the actuator to spring-return; the actuator cannot exhaust itself of air. It requires a controller, which consumes air in sensing and maintaining pneumatic equilibrium within itself, or it requires an EP, which does not consume air, to direct pneumatic signal to it before it can react and move its damper or valve. Whether or not a device is an air-consuming device has to do with the normal "bleed" or discharge of a small amount of "pilot" air normally occurring in pneumatic thermostats, humidistats, pressurestats, controllers, etc. as a necessary function that permits pilot chamber pressure regulation by a lever or bimetal. As temperature or pressure changes, the "leakport" is allowed to bleed either less or more, thereby changing the pilot chamber pressure, which in turn operates the branch line feed valve to send either more or less air to the actuator under control. This build-up of branch line air pressure is "fed back" to the pilot chamber so equalization may occur, and the actuator may be positioned properly in response to sensor demands. So it is the air-consuming devices that we need to consider as we begin the selection process for our air compressor.

Once total air consumption in CFM is known, an air compressor, whose delivery exceeds that figure, can be selected. For maximum compressor life, a unit is selected so that its run time is equal to or less than its off time, permitting sufficiently long rest periods for the unit in between pumping requirement cycles. Receiver size determines the length of run and rest periods, and it should be large enough to prevent "short cycling," frequent stopping and starting, which is harmful to the compressor motor and tends to shorten the life of the motor starter. Compressor manufacturers publish necessary selection data to be used in determining the best size of compressor for the installation.

Only "instrument-grade" air-compressing outfits should be used in temperature control work, unless plant air is available from an industrial compressor, and the necessary filtering, oil-entrapment, and moisture removal equipment is used. Compressors designed for use in temperature control work are manufactured with closer tolerances to help ensure less oil contamination of the air supply. Oil-free compressors, requiring no oil for lubrication, are available, also.

Air is stored in the receiver at high pressure and reduced through pressure-reducing valves for system usage. Normal cut-in pressure for the compressor might be 70lb, and normal cut-out pressure for the compressor might be 90lb. A pressure switch, sensing tank or receiver pressure, starts and stops the compressor. A relief valve, set perhaps at 125lb, is installed to prevent overpressurizing the receiver should the

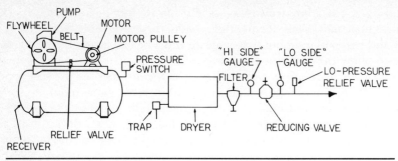

Figure 30   Air compressor.

pressure switch fail for any reason to stop the compressor. When the compressor stops, an unloader acts to take pressure off the cylinder heads of the compressor, so that when restarting is called for, the unit may start without pressure on the head of the cylinder for unloaded starting.

Tank air, after being dehumidified and filtered, is piped through a reducing station, which steps the air pressure down to that suitable for the controls (usually 20lb, or so). A low-pressure relief valve is installed after the reducing station set for 25lb to ensure that overpressurization of the controls does not occur, for this would result in damage to the system's components which are not rated for high pressures.

Dehumidification of the air at high pressure ensures maximum moisture removal. "Dry" air is necessary to prevent fouling or scale buildup within instruments, and to prevent water from developing within the piping system from condensation. A temperature-pressure relationship exists relative to the ability of air to hold moisture, or water vapor. Cold temperatures cause water vapor in air to condense in the form of water, and pressurization of air lowers its capacity to retain water vapor. We use these two factors together in a refrigerated air dryer which "processes" the air at high pressure, condensing the moisture from it, so that should it be exposed to cold temperatures in the piping system at lower pressure after passing through the reducing station, no condensation will form which would damage our controls. The refrigerated air dryer cools the air, causing condensation intentionally, and then traps it and dumps it to a drain.

As illustrated in Figure 30, the principal components of our air compressor are (1) the electric motor, (2) the piston pump and flywheel, (3) receiver or tank, and (4) pressure switch. These are usually assembled as a unit. In addition, a v-groove belt is provided between the motor and pump, and perhaps a belt guard and motor starter. A relief valve is usually preinstalled on the unit, as well.

6

Air - Handler Control Applications

FRESH AIR CONSIDERATIONS

As we begin now to examine the applications of automatic temperature controls, it would seem appropriate to begin with the air handler, because it is the source of our heating and cooling air supply, and because its controls are so closely tied to maintaining comfortable occupied space temperatures.

We will start with a look at the mixing dampers on the intake side of the unit and the mixed air plenum. Consider Figure 31, and note the relationship of the fresh air and return air dampers and the resultant converging air streams that establish the quality for the mixed air entering the filter bank.

The quality of the control air dampers cannot be regarded lightly, as poor-quality dampers can cause operational difficulties. Loose-fitting blades permit leakage, which upsets air balancing and often introduces excessive cold air from the outside during periods of shutdown. Good dampers, squarely installed, with tight-fitting blades, weather stripping, and smooth-working, substantial linkages are necessary for maintenance of predetermined temperatures in the mixed air plenum.

Economizer Controls

Outdoor air, at certain temperatures, represents a building owner's most economical source of cooling. Figure 32 shows how controls would be applied to take advantage of "free cooling" when the outdoor air was capable of producing mixed air temperatures suitable for cooling, for large units serving multiple areas.

Temperature transmitter TT-1 (see Figure 32), located so as to sense the outdoor air temperature, sends a linear signal to controller C-1,

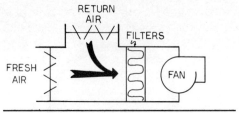

Figure 31   Air-mixing plenum—converging air streams.

whose setpoint may be 60°. Temperature transmitter TT-2, located so as to sense the mixed air temperature about to flow through the air handler and to be delivered to the conditioned spaces, sends a linear signal to controller C-2, whose setpoint is also 60°. Both controllers are capable of picking out information from the linear signal that tells them when their setpoints are being exceeded.

Controller C-2 is direct acting, which means that on a rise in pressure signal from TT-2, which correlates with a rise in sensed temperature, C-2 will increase its output, which passes through C-1. C-1 is reverse acting, so that on a rise in pressure signal from TT-1, which, again, correlates with a rise in sensed temperature, C-1 will decrease its output, which is merely a "passing on" of the signal it received from C-2. In this manner, C-1 may "override" C-2 to prevent passage of C-2's signal. This limiting action is important, as we shall see, in that C-1 has the responsibility to determine when the outdoor air temperature is too high to be used for maintenance of a 60° air temperature, suitable for cooling.

Assuming an outdoor air temperature below 60°, and a mixed air temperature above 60°, a controller signal from C-2 passes through C-1

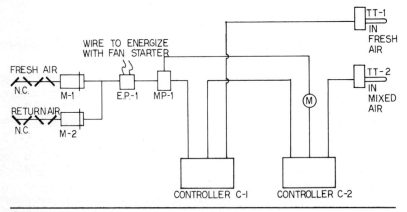

Figure 32   Typical economizer control loop.

and enters the "pilot" port of minimum-positioning relay MP-1. MP-1 is present to hold open the fresh air damper just enough to introduce into the unit a minimum amount of fresh air at all times when the fan is running. This ensures that a stagnant air condition does not develop within the conditioned spaces, and that code minimum fresh air requirements for occupied spaces are met. Upon seeing a signal from C-1 greater than its "preset" output, MP-1 will pass it on, allowing its preset minimum output to be "overridden." Accordingly, when mixed air conditions require it, and outside air temperature permits it, the minimum position of the fresh air damper is "overridden" to introduce greater amounts of fresh air and lesser amounts of return air to lower the mixed air temperature.

Electro-pneumatic relay EP-1 (see Figure 32), which is an electrically actuated solenoid air valve, is interposed in the line between MP-1 and the "motorized" damper actuators M-1 and M-2. EP-1 is wired into the air handler fan motor starter, so as to be energized and pass the air signal when the fan motor starter is energized. This is so that the fresh air damper actuator will be "exhausted" of its air signal when the unit fan is off, and by spring return will position the fresh air damper to its "normally closed" position. Conversely, the return air damper actuator is exhausted of its air signal, too, when the fan is off, and its damper returns to the "normally open" position. This prevents the migration of cold fresh air into the unit at night when the fan is off, with the resultant danger of freezing the heating or cooling coils which utilize hot or chilled water.

M-1 and M-2 are piston-type louver actuators and are spring-loaded to return to their normal positions when the air signal is removed. When air is applied, the force of the spring is overcome, and the piston "strokes", applying force to the crankarm on the dampers, positioning them accordingly.

EP-1 is positioned just before the actuators, so that it can remove all signal from them, regardless of the outputs of controllers or minimum positioning relay.

On a rise in mixed air temperature, C-2 will call for opening of the fresh air damper and closing of the return-air damper in order to get as much fresh air as it needs to maintain 60°. But above a 60° outside air temperature, C-1 will overcall C-2, and return the dampers to their preset minimum. Thus, the introduction of fresh air which is too warm for cooling is prevented, and now mechanical means for cooling must be started. Remembering the motor control section we discussed earlier, it might be that at 60°, a separate outdoor air thermostat will start the chilled water pump and associated pieces of equipment so we may now have chilled water available at the chilled water coil in the air handler for the purpose of handling the cooling load, for which the outdoor air is no longer suitable.

In the wintertime, when outdoor air temperatures are very cold, "low-limit" action is also provided by C-2 because it will back off on fresh air and introduce more return air if the mixed air temperature begins to fall below C-2's setpoint. This action serves to protect the downstream water coils from dangerously low, freezing temperatures. In this connection, TT-2 should be a sensor with an averaging element, strung back and forth across the cross-sectional area of the plenum, rather than a rigid stem insertion sensor, unable to sense air temperatures all across the plenum. The first concern in applying sensors is to ensure that the controlled medium is properly sensed, and for this reason, in very large plenums, it may be necessary to use two sensors, both with averaging elements, and to pipe their outputs into a low-pressure selector relay, so that the coldest temperature sensed can be permitted to control the fresh air for maximum "low-limiting" action.

Different plenum situations and damper arrangements can create potentially dangerous air flow developments, known as stratification or laminar air flow. This occurs when the converging fresh and return airstreams do not "squirrel up," or become properly mixed. The resultant laminated air stream produces different temperatures of air entering the flow stream across the water coils. Potential freezeup conditions exist if a layer of this air is at or below 32°, particularly if water in one or more of the coils is not moving, as it would not be in a chilled water coil which was shut down for the winter. This points up, again, the need for good cross-sectional sampling of the plenum air by one or more sensors capable of detecting the coldest and most potentially dangerous air stream temperature.

Laminar air flow can be guarded against by careful selection of automatic dampers and arrangement so that the opening of the blades begins to introduce its air flow into the air coming through the other damper. Sometimes, even this doesn't prevent stratification, so baffles or fabricated turbulators of some design must be used to scramble the air.

Upslant deflectors angled at 45° have to be used in cases where the fresh air enters the fresh air damper at its lowest point and travels across a relatively flat plenum, sneaking over the bottom edge of the filter bank, and continuing on, undisturbed, to where it reaches the bottom row of a water coil. Fairly flat plenums with the lower edges of their fresh air dampers level with the plenum's bottom are frequently good candidates for upslant deflectors. Extremely cold outside air temperatures quickly reveal thermal stratification and point up the need for corrective action. Wintertime is when stratification or laminar air flow begins to become evident.

A further refinement and improvement on decision making by automatic controls as to when to use outdoor air is introduction of fresh air based on enthalpy, or total heat content of the air. Temperature and relative humidity sensors located both in the outside air and return air transmit signals to "total heat" controllers, which, through comparison relays, are used to make the decision to "go on outside air" when the total heat of the fresh air is less than the total heat of the returning air. In this way, both sensible and latent heat content of the air is taken into consideration, resulting in "smarter" decisions and better control for the building's owner and occupants.

The return air temperature might be 75°, and the fresh air might be 65°, but if the outside air were "muggy," or heavily saturated with moisture, the "total heat" of the fresh air would most likely be higher than the return air, so the continued use of return air with just a minimum amount of fresh air would be the better decision. Of course, mechanical cooling would have to be put into effect to provide cooling. Changing over to "free cooling" based on temperature alone would have been a mistake; the total heat content of the air was too high.

In larger systems, a relief damper would be sequenced with the fresh air and return air dampers, which would "relieve" the building of excessive air and static pressure when free cooling was being utilized. The motion of the relief damper would track the fresh air damper, and as the fresh air damper moved on beyond its minimum, the relief damper would open accordingly, while the return damper closed a proportionate amount, thereby balancing fresh air flow into and used air flow out of the building.

Positive positioning devices for damper actuators are readily available, and they serve to ensure damper movement proportionate to controller signal, if size of damper or sluggishness of linkage response is encountered. By using a piloting device on the pneumatic actuator, capable of comparing actuator stroke with the linearity of the incoming controller signal, it can apply full main line pressure to the actuator, if necessary, in order to get the proper movement necessary to cancel the call for the application of main air pressure to the diaphragm of the actuator. This is accomplished by control manufacturers in different ways, but basically it consists of mechanically monitoring damper actuator stroke and feeding back this mechanical movement to the pneumatic piloting mechanism, which controls the high-pressure input port.

Fixed Quantity Fresh Air Controls

Some air handler applications, notably kitchen fresh-air makeup and hospital clean-room areas, require 100 percent fresh air with no recirculation of return air. In these cases, fresh air dampers open fully on fan startup, and interlocked exhaust fans dump the air from the conditioned spaces on a "once-through" basis. Notice in Figure 33 that EP-1 puts main air on damper motor M-1. No intermediary controller modulates the fresh-air damper. The motor starter control circuit is utilized through a maintained start switch to energize EP-1. The motor starter will not energize until end switch ES closes its contact, indicating that the fresh air damper is 100 percent open. Freeze-proof steam-preheat coil PHC tempers the incoming air under control of temperature controller TC-1, set for probably 55°. Control valve V-1 will modulate in response to TC-1 to maintain its setpoint. Freeze protection thermostat FZ-1 is a safety, designed to stop the fan by deenergizing EP-1, closing damper D-1, and dropping out the starter should it sense temperatures near freezing. FZ-1 utilizes a capillary sensitive to the coldest single foot of element along its 20-foot length. Space thermostat T-1 can sequence control valves V-2 and V-3 to introduce chilled water or hot water to the respective chilled water and hot water coils to maintain space temperature. Firestat FS-1 located in the discharge will stop the fan by dropping out the motor starter should it sense temperatures approaching its setpoint, which might indicate the presence of fire in the unit. Filter banks are omitted for clarity. Cross-hatched lines indicate electrical wiring and number of wires.

Care needs to be taken in the selection of the firestat so that its setpoint is not below warm air temperatures which may be expected to be encountered coming off the heating coil when T-1 is calling for heating. Most codes allow firestat setpoints to be at least 50° above high ambient.

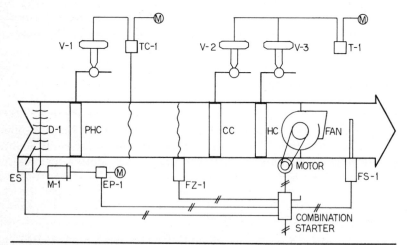

Figure 33 One hundred percent fresh air unit.

When chilled water is off in the wintertime, TC-1 will be maintaining 55°—air suitable for cooling—so when T-1 modulates V-3 closed, the 55° tempered air will be permitted to flow on through the unit for cooling of conditioned spaces.

Sequencing of V-2 and V-3 is accomplished through the use of different spring ranges. V-3 would be normally open, requiring air signal from T-1 to close the valve, with a spring range of perhaps of 3 to 8lb, while V-2 would be normally closed, requiring air signal from T-1 to open the valve, with a spring range of perhaps 9 to 13lb. In this way, increasing pneumatic signal from direct-acting thermostat T-1, piped to both valves, would first close V-3 to heating, and on a further rise in space temperature, open V-2 to cooling.

On a loss of main air pressure to the controls, M-1 would lose its signal and begin to close damper D-1, which in turn would open end switch ES and drop out the fan starter to stop the fan. Since a loss of air would close the damper, we must stop the fan to prevent its pulling against a closed damper. Also, heating valves V-1 and V-3 would fail to their normally open position, so severe overheating would occur should we continue with fan operation.

Should automatic starting of the fan be desired, say from a timeclock, we would utilize the "auto" leg of the "hand-off-auto" switch, and connect it through damper end switch ES. The clock, then, would energize EP-1 to initiate startup. The "hand" position would be connected to energize EP-1, also, rather than to energize the starter directly, because we must first open the fresh air damper.

Since this is a fresh-air unit, sizing of the cooling coil would have to allow for the introduction of very humid and warm air in the summertime, as it would have to be able to remove considerable sensible and latent heat from the air before it could be introduced into the spaces to be conditioned.

Summer-Winter Changeover

We have discussed returning the fresh air damper to a minimum position through the use of a local outside air temperature sensor. Owing to variations in setpoints or slightly varying conditions at the outside air temperature sensors for the various air handlers, we might find that the fresh air dampers on each unit were not all being minimum-positioned at the same time, and this may be a problem, if mechanical generation of chilled water is being started at the same setpoint. Frequently, changeover of the air handler fresh air damper control mode is tied to startup of chilled water equipment, and this ensures that all air handlers have their respective fresh air dampers set for minimum when chilled water is delivered to the cooling coil in the air handler. In this manner, unnecessary loading of the chilled water coil with warm, perhaps moist, outside air is prevented, and unnecessary energy consumption required to cool excessive outside air quantities is circumvented.

In central changeover systems, one thermostat, strategically located in the outside air, is selected to initiate entire system changeover. This can be accomplished through the use of switching relays, located at the various air handlers and indexed from a central changeover signal. Consider Figure 34, which details how such a central changeover system might work. A manual "heat-auto-cool" selector switch is provided, to allow owner discretion, as to whether system changeover will be left to be accomplished automatically or "locked in" to a preferred mode. Temperature transmitter TT-1, located in the outside air, sends its signal to changeover controller C-1, which, at a predetermined temperature signal, two-positions itself in a direct acting mode to increase its branch output to selector switch S-1. When S-1 is indexed to the "automatic" position, ports 2 and C are connected, and output from C-1 is passed through to changeover air valve AV-1. On an increase in signal to AV-1, it strokes to connect ports C and NC, so that main air pressure is applied to all changeover relays CO-1 at the various air handlers. Other automatic devices to start chilled water generation equipment are indexed at the same time.

When CO-1 receives a changeover signal, it connects ports C and NC, thereby exhausting the control signal from MP-1, causing M-1 to assume its minimum position.

MP-1 permits adjustment of the minimum of the fresh air damper so the quantity can be fine-tuned to provide just enough to meet code

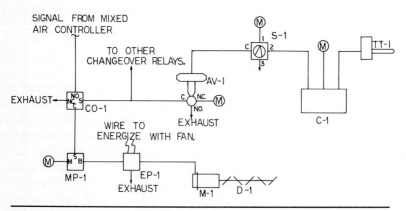

Figure 34   Central changeover of fresh air damper control.

fresh-air requirements, while contributing minimally to loading of the chilled water or direct expansion cooling coil.

Mode selector switch S-1 furnishes the building's operator with the option of keeping the system indexed for mechanical cooling or continuously indexed for free cooling. These switch positions might be labeled "Summer" and "Winter," respectively. In the "Summer" mode, switch ports 1 and C are connected, and constant main holds changeover valve AV-1 positioned to send main to all changeover relays CO-1, thereby exhausting signal from air handler minimum position switches. In the "winter" mode, AV-1 remains "normal," since switch ports C and 3 are connected, and changeover relays CO-1 do not index to exhaust signal from MP-1.

Mechanical cooling system PE relays, for starting pumps and energizing refrigeration equipment, would be indexed from the same changeover signal from AV-1.

Day-Night Changeover

We can see from the foregoing discussions of fresh air and minimum fresh air that our concentration has been on assuring that some fresh air is taken into the building when the fan is in operation, both summer and winter. But during periods when the building is not occupied, evenings, weekends, and holidays, there is no necessity for introducing even the minimum amount of fresh air, because there are no occupants. In the wintertime, particularly, inefficiencies result from unnecessarily heating outside air drawn into the building if it is not needed. So at night and other unoccupied times, we want to close off the outside air damper so no fresh air is introduced. A popular method for accomplishing this is the 7-day timeclock. In Figure 35 our timeclock will energize our central day-night EP at night, causing it to deliver main air to night thermostats and switching relays. The switching relay takes signal from our fresh air damper actuator, and it "spring-returns" the damper to the closed position. At the same time, our system return air damper would open fully. Our night thermostat, upon receiving main air, passes it on to our normally closed PE relay, because the night thermostat is direct acting, and the space temperature is above its setpoint. This causes our PE to open its contact, and stop the fan. The fan will remain off until space temperature falls to within the setting of the night thermostat, at which time the PE will be allowed to reclose, starting the fan. By this time, our day thermostats throughout the building will be cold and will have their actuators positioned for full heating. The fan would remain on, until space temperature rose to the setting of the night thermostat, at which

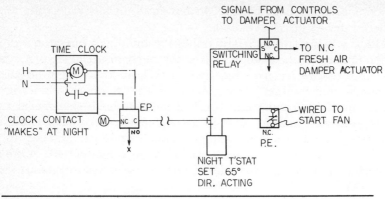

Figure 35   Day-night changeover.

time, the fan would be shut down again. Thus, we say we cycle the system fan at night to maintain reduced space temperatures with all outdoor air closed off.

When our time clock indexes to "day" next morning, the EP will remove all air from our day-night changeover control loop, and the fan PEs will close to run the fans continuously during the day. At the same time, switching relays will return control of the fresh air (and return air) dampers to the air handling unit controls. Fresh air will be introduced into the building during the day.

Frequently, day-night changeover loops are "zoned," and provisions are made for zone override of night setback, in case portions of the building are desired to be used at night. In this instance, two-position pneumatic switches could be installed between the central day-night EP and night thermostats and switching relays. Normally, the switches would be left indexed to pass air straight through, but during periods when it was desirable to override the timeclock for a specific zone, the switch would be opened, and exhaust air from its respective night thermostat and switching relays, causing the fan to start and the fresh air damper to assume its daytime operational mode.

Most seven-day timeclocks used in temperature control work incorporate an override lever to permit manually changing the position of the clock's contacts. Dial trippers can be set to trip the clock's contacts at different times, subject to a schedule that suits the building's management. Optional spring reserve is a feature offered by most manufacturers, and this ensures the clock's time-keeping-mechanism operation when power is lost for up to 24 hours. This way, a power outage will not cause the timeclock to lose time, and necessitate resetting.

COOLING AND DEHUMIDIFICATION

During the summertime, when outside air temperatures are high, and relative humidity reaches uncomfortable proportions, the air handler's air conditioning efforts are directed toward cooling and dehumidifying the air being processed through it, so that it can be made suitable for delivery to the conditioned spaces to maintain space temperatures. The air temperature must be lowered, and moisture must be removed. Directing the air across a chilled coil serves both of these purposes. Air temperatures across the cooling coil may drop as much as 30°. When this happens, the dewpoint of the air is reached, and moisture condenses out on the coil. As moisture is condensed out of the air, its dewpoint is lowered by virtue of the fact that it has less moisture to give up, and it has greater capacity to absorb moisture when once again it finds its temperature elevated after being delivered to the conditioned spaces or reheated. Thus, the air is dehumidified, cooled, and, in a sense, reconditioned for redelivery to the areas under control.

Maintenance of cooling coil discharge temperatures is a very prevalent form of control found in both central fan and multizone unit applications. This assures cool air temperatures necessary for cooling any portion of the area being served, and in a central fan system, provisions are usually made for reheating the delivered air if an area subcools. In a multizone unit, zone thermostats can blend quantities of cold deck and hot deck air as necessary.

A cold deck sensor, with averaging element, is installed to sense the temperature of the air coming off the cooling coil. Its output will be piped to a receiver controller, and the controller may modulate a chilled water coil control valve. Readout of the cold deck temperature is often desirable, and it is an efficient byproduct of the linear signal already being supplied by the cold deck sensor. By installing a pneumatic readout gauge in the receiving port of the controller, we can have continuous indication of our cold deck temperature in the air handler. The gauge would be fitted with a graduated dial whose range matches that of our sensor. Note in Figure 36 that we have also added a sensor in the outside air, whose function is to provide reset signal to receiver controller RC-1. As per the reset schedule, our cold deck temperature control point would drop from 65° at 65° outside air temperature, to 55° at 85° outside air temperature. In this manner, we introduce some economy into our chilled water system by not calling for the maintenance of 55° until outside air conditions begin to necessitate it.

Our receiver controller is direct acting, so on a rise in signal from TT-1, indicating a rise in cold deck temperature, RC-1 will increase its

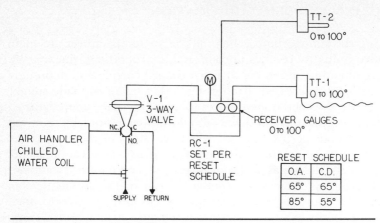

Figure 36   Control of chilled water coil.

output to three-way valve V-1, causing it to modulate for a greater flow of chilled water to the coil. The direct-acting topworks will move the valve stem downward, and the normally open port will be throttled back while the normally closed port will be throttled open.

A direct expansion refrigerant coil would be handled differently. Trying to maintain a coil-discharge temperature frequently results in short cycling of the refrigerant compressor and is not recommended by many manufacturers. The more practical approach is to allow the decision for cooling to be made by a thermostat having the greatest need for cooling, which will start the compressor and permit the refrigerant circuit to operate under its own head pressure controls. For this control scheme, we would use a selector relay to judge which thermostat had the greatest need for cooling, based on the highest signal coming from all thermostats. This highest signal would be piped to a PE relay, which would energize the refrigerant control circuit.

HEATING

As the leaves turn, and the days cool, our need for cooling begins to give way to a need for heating. On the larger central fan systems which we have been discussing, a preheat coil may be employed to ensure minimum entering outside air temperatures during cold days. As mentioned previously, the central fan system employing a cooling coil designed to maintain cool discharge air temperatures, usually has reheats in space to temper the air during the cooling season. This continues to hold true in the winter, but the chiller is off, and we are using outside air for maintenance of these cool discharge air temperatures during the winter. However, given a need for cooling during the wintertime, we could run the risk of bringing in outside air that is too cold, and when we have established a minimum quantity of outside air necessary for fresh air requirements, we need to condition this minimum amount to prevent it from becoming a freezeup hazard. So the first step in treating this outside air would be in the form of a preheat coil as discussed in the earlier section of this book which dealt with the 100 percent fresh air unit, only this time our preheat coil would be located in the mixed air, to take advantage of warming of the incoming fresh air with return air. And assuming a low limit in the mixed air which would bring the fresh air damper all the way back to minimum, if necessary, to prevent freezing temperatures from entering the unit, our preheat coil would come into play only if the entering minimum fresh air, when mixed with return air, was still too cold.

Note Figure 37, which shows the preheat coil placed in the air handler, and located in the mixed air, to provide final tempering treatment, if necessary, to the air stream, before it reaches the chilled water coil, which now, of course, is idle. The preheat coil controller becomes the final safety (except for the freezestat, which would shut the fan down and require reset) in assuring safe entering air temperatures. Preheat coil control could easily be in the form of a sensor and receiver controller, but here we have selected a self-contained controller, with capillary and remote averaging bulb. Remembering the application of controller C-2

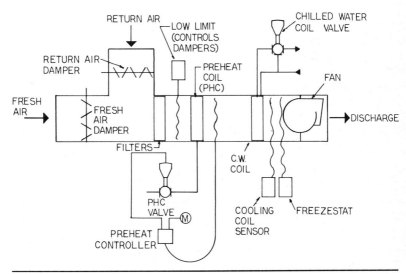

Figure 37   Preheat coil in central fan system.

in our economizer control loop discussed earlier in this book (Figure 32), our low limit here would be looking for 60° minimum and would back off on fresh air, until the fresh air damper was at minimum. Our preheat controller, then, might be set at 50°, somewhat below the low limit, to prevent the use of heating energy until absolutely necessary.

Heating and Ventilating Unit

Many areas of commercial and industrial buildings are selected to be served by air handlers that provide heating and ventilation only and do not offer cooling. Vocational training shop areas of high schools or trade schools are frequently handled this way, as well as many gymnasiums. Storage and locker areas often are not judged as necessary candidates for cooling, as well as automotive and truck repair areas. In these cases, the HVAC designer may select heating and ventilating units to serve their temperature control requirements.

Quite often, the fans in these units are started manually, whenever the area they serve is in use, or these "H & V" units could be interlocked with exhaust fans in the area, or to lighting controls, which indicate occupancy. In any case, the H & V unit will usually be controlled from a space thermostat, which will sequence the heating coil with the ventilation dampers. A night thermostat may override the H & V unit's shutdown at night for maintenance of minimum space temperatures.

In Figure 38, we show an electric heating coil with four stages, with

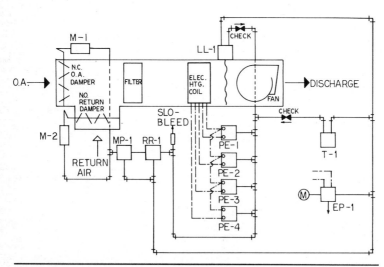

Figure 38   Heating and ventilating unit.

PEs set to deenergize all of the stages before opening the fresh air damper beyond minimum in order to obtain ventilation for cooling purposes. Note the discharge low limit LL-1, piped into the control circuit to override the space thermostat, as may be necessary, to prevent excessively low discharge temperatures when the space thermostat is calling for "no heat" and ventilation. Also, the space thermostat is reverse acting, so the electric heating coil would "fail safe" to the "off" position in the event of loss of compressed air to the control system. No freezestat is installed, because there is no water coil which could be endangered by freezing air temperatures. Our EP, wired into the fan starter, takes air off our pneumatic controls, which deenergizes the electric heating, closes the fresh air damper, and opens the return air damper.

When the fan is started, EP-1 sends air to the unit control system. On a rise in space temperature, reverse-acting space thermostat T-1 decreases its "branch line" pressure (output) to allow normally open PE relays 1 through 4 to open in sequence to deenergize the electric heating in four stages. Reverse-acting low limit LL-1 can overcall T-1, by increasing its output on a fall in discharge temperature to its setpoint. Branch line check valves prevent feedback from LL-1 to T-1, or vice versa. An adjustable slow bleed prevents "locked-in" branch pressure to the PEs and RR-1. Reversing relay RR-1 converts low signal to the PEs, indicating a need to deenergize heating, to a high signal to override minimum position relay MP-1, to modulate the fresh air damper open and the return air damper closed for ventilation to the space.

Spring ranges of damper motors M-1 and M-2 could be 9 to 13lb, so as to be on the "high end" of the direct-acting signal (from RR-1). This would be the reverse equivalent of the "low end" of the reverse-acting signal from T-1. PEs 1 through 4 could be set to open on a falling signal from 14 to 10lb, equivalent to a rising temperature at T-1.

Our night thermostat (not shown in Figure 38) would override the unit "off" switch to cycle the fan for reduced space temperatures. In that case, it would be desireable to add a clock-controlled EP between MP-1 and damper motors M-1 and M-2, to close off fresh air during the night.

Heating, Ventilating, and Cooling Unit

When multiple central-station units are used for space conditioning, they will usually handle the year-round heating and cooling requirements of the spaces they serve without additional terminal units for final treatment of the air being delivered. Each, then, should be able to provide fresh air ventilation for natural or "free" cooling when outdoor air temperatures are suitable, and mechanical cooling when necessary, as well as heating. These units could easily be controlled from room thermostats, each one completely controlling its respective air handler, through the sequenced stages of heating, ventilating, and cooling.

In Figure 39, we see room thermostat T-1 piped to control valves and dampers. T-1 is direct acting, and on a rise in room temperature, T-1 increases its output through low limit LL-1 to modulate heating hot water valve V-1 toward the closed position. Should room temperature continue to rise, the increasing signal from T-1 modulates M-1 to open the fresh air damper and close the return air damper, and then, if necessary, modulate cooling chilled water valve V-2 toward the open position.

In the event air temperature off the heating coil starts to drop below LL-1's setpoint of 50°, it will overcall T-1, to assume control of M-1 and V-1 to maintain its setpoint.

EP-1, wired into the fan starter, removes air from minimum positioning switch MP-1, to close the fresh air damper whenever the fan is off. Changeover relay CO-1 locks out thermostat T-1's signal above a certain outdoor air temperature to return the fresh air damper to its minimum position during fan operation.

In the summertime, LL-1 is unaffected by cool air temperatures off the chilled water coil, owing to its location "before the coil" in terms of air-flow, so T-1 can fully open V-2 for full cooling as required.

Spring ranges of the valves and damper operator might be as follows, to obtain the desired sequencing: normally open V-1, 2 to 5lb; normally closed fresh air damper operator M-1, 6 to 9lb; normally closed V-2, 10

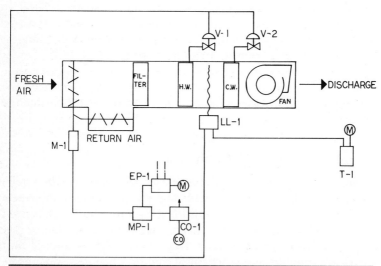

Figure 39   Central station heating, ventilating, and cooling unit.

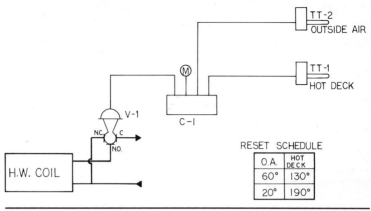

Figure 40   Hot deck reset from outside air.

to 13lb. Thus, an increasing pneumatic signal from room thermostat T-1 can sequence the air conditioning unit through heating, ventilating, and cooling, making all three modes of space conditioning responsive to the one room thermostat.

HOT DECK RESET IN MULTIZONE UNIT

In multizone units, where room thermostats blend quantities of warm and cool air at the unit for delivery to their respective zones, it is advisable to reschedule hot deck temperatures being maintained, inversely with space demands, or outside air temperatures. Remembering our earlier discussion concerning reset schedule control of a chilled water coil, we shall now examine a typical reset schedule and control scheme for a hot water heating coil in the hot deck of a multizone unit, elevating the hot deck temperature setpoint as the outside air temperature falls, or as room temperatures dictate.

In Figure 40, direct-acting controller C-1 will modulate valve V-1 toward the coil bypass position on a rise in hot deck temperature at transmitter TT-1. As the outside air temperature rises as sensed by transmitter TT-2, the scheduled hot deck temperature will be lowered in accordance with the reset schedule. This method of hot deck temperature control utilizes outside air temperature as the governing factor in determining what the hot deck temperature should be.

To permit reset by space temperature demands, Figure 40 would be modified, as shown in Figure 41. Now, low signal selector LS-1 will allow the coldest of the three space thermostats T-1, T-2, or T-3 to reschedule

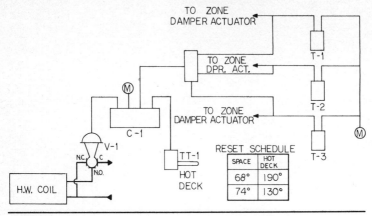

Figure 41   Hot deck reset from coldest space stat.

hot deck temperatures in accordance with the reset schedule. Direct acting controller C-1 operates our valve V-1 as before.

FACE AND BYPASS COIL
CAPACITY CONTROL

Our previous discussions, regarding water coil capacity control, have concerned themselves with control valves, used to regulate water flow through the coil. Another method of coil capacity control utilizes a damper actuator and control dampers, installed so that as one damper opens to admit air to flow across the water coil another closes to limit the amount of air which can bypass the coil. This method of control for a water coil is known as "face and bypass."

A heating coil in a heating and ventilating unit might be piped for wild flow of hot water through the coil. Within the unit, factory-installed face and bypass dampers are linked together so that a pneumatic actuator may be installed to a common drive shaft, so as to regulate air flow within. The spring-loaded actuator is connected so that it may be controlled by a direct-acting space thermostat, modulating the face damper closed on a rise in space temperature and the bypass damper open. In this connection, the face damper would be normally open, and the bypass damper would be normally closed.

In Figure 42, space thermostat T-1 acts on a rise in temperature to modulate M-1 to close the face damper and open the bypass damper, subject to overcall by low limit LL-1. A restrictor (res., Figure 42) in the output line of thermostat T-1 allows single-pipe low limit LL-1 to bleed the line on a fall in temperature below its setpoint to bring M-1 back as

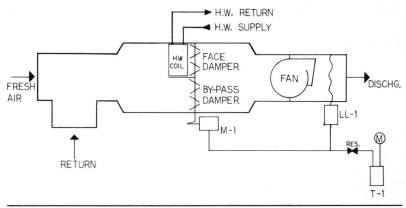

Figure 42   Heating and ventilating unit, face and bypass control of heating coil.

much as may be required to maintain a minimum discharge temperature as set at LL-1.

Sometimes a two-position control valve will be added and arranged to close off flow to the coil when the face damper is fully closed. This could be accomplished by a diverting relay piped to switch main air on and off to the control valve, and indexed by thermostat T-1. The diverting relay would be set to actuate at the high end of T-1's range.

DUCT PRESSURE CONTROL

No discussion of air handler controls would be complete without giving consideration to duct pressure controls, which are finding increasing application, as today's larger systems make use of the energy saving technique of modulating fan capacities, as terminal units in variable volume air handling systems throttle their output in response to space temperatures.

Variable air volume systems employ terminal units out in space, which effect cooling for the spaces they serve by opening up for a greater flow of cool air on a space temperature rise. Assuming a warm building, most of the terminal units would be positioned for maximum flow of cool air from the duct system to the spaces. A variable-volume fan in the air handler must be able to deliver the needed air for cooling. As the spaces cool down, the terminal units will throttle back on the amount of air they require. The fan in the air handler must be able to decrease its output, or run the risk of overpressurizing the duct system, which could lead to noisy units, poor temperature control, and perhaps even duct damage.

Additionally, the fan would be wasting electrical power in its attempt to deliver air which the duct system does not now need. So fans installed in air conditioning systems which make use of reduced CFM requirements when the cooling load is down need to be designed for fan capacity reduction controls.

Two major types of fans designed for this purpose are (1) vaneaxial fans with variable pitch blades and (2) centrifugal fans with variable inlet vanes. Both are fitted with actuators which can modulate either the variable pitch blades or the variable inlet vanes in response to duct pressure sensors and controls. Both result in power reduction requirements to the electric motor driving the fan when the air volume requirements decrease and help the building's owners save operating dollars.

Vaneaxial fans induce air flow axially and discharge it axially. Hub-mounted blades, travelling at high speed, have their pitch varied from roughly 45° at full pitch, or maximum flow, to nearly 0° at minimum pitch, or minimum flow. The variable-pitch actuator is mounted on the top or side of the round fan casing and operates a control lever, which penetrates the casing to reach the blades variable-pitch gearbox.

Centrifugal fans induce air flow axially but discharge it tangentially. Inlet-mounted vanes which are stationary are opened and closed from nearly full open to full closed. They open, generally, at an angle which compliments the rotation of the fan, to aid in guiding the air in the direction the fan is already rotating. The variable-inlet actuator is mounted off to the side, and a control rod imparts movement to the vane cluster.

When system return fans are used, they usually are of the variable-capacity type also, so that their capacity can be modulated in concordance with the supply fan.

In Figure 43, we see the two types of fans, predominantly used where modulated fan capacity control is required. The pneumatic actuators are inside the air handler's casing but are outside the fan's impeller chamber. Generally, the actuators will require high pressure main air in addition to the regulated air signal from the controller, because they may have industrial type, pilot positioning devices.

A normal mode of fan capacity control might utilize total pressure transmitters located two thirds of the way down the longest duct run on various floors, piped into a lowest pressure selector relay that allows the transmitter most in need of additional pressure to reset an industrial total pressure discharge controller, subject to a discharge duct, static pressure high limit, set in accordance with the fan manufacturer's directions. A return fan in this air handling system would be controlled from an industrial type, velocity-pressure controller, reset by discharge fan velocity pressure. Sensing tips in the ductwork would be piped for total

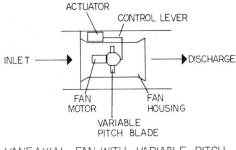

VANEAXIAL FAN WITH VARIABLE PITCH BLADES

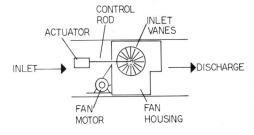

CENTRIFUGAL FAN WITH VARIABLE INLET VANES

Figure 43   Central fan capacity control methods.

pressure or velocity pressure, as the application might require, and be connected to industrial-type transmitters, whose pressure sensing elements have been selected for the appropriate range involved.

Note the control diagram, Figure 44. Supply fan total pressure transmitter TP-1 pilots the signal port of total pressure controller TPC-1. Remote duct total pressure transmitter TP-2 inputs to low-pressure selector LPS-1, which pilots the reset port of TPC-1. TPC-1 outputs to fan capacity controller actuator M-1, subject to overcall by static high limit SHL-1. Setup for TPC-1 would be in pounds of air, 3 to 15lb, because of the receiver elements, which are receiving a 3- to 15-lb signal from the transmitters. Readout, however, on TPC-1 would be in inches of water.

Return fan velocity pressure transmitter VP-1 (Figure 44) pilots the signal port of velocity pressure controller VPC-1. Supply fan velocity pressure transmitter VP-2 pilots the reset port of VPC-1. VPC-1 outputs to fan capacity controller actuator M-1. Return fan velocity pressure will track the supply fan on a reset schedule as designated by the HVAC

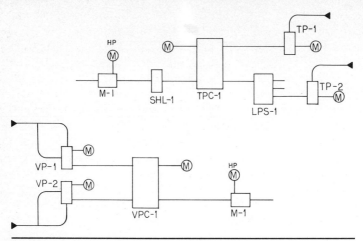

Figure 44   Fan capacity control diagrams.

designer so that proper pressurization of the supply fan suction mixing plenum is preserved.

Greater emphasis will continue to be placed on accurate management of fan discharge pressures in variable air volume systems, which will necessitate the selection of highly stable sensors and controllers for application in these systems. Control manufacturers' industrial-quality lines offer devices with the quality and integrity required. Achieving smooth, stable control responses in static pressure systems is the control application designer's goal.

SPACE RELATIVE HUMIDITY CONTROL

One final air treatment consideration needs to be dealt with before the air leaving the air handler is delivered to the conditioned spaces being served. In the wintertime, when it is quite cold, substantial heating of the air passing through the unit is probably taking place. With minimum outdoor air being introduced, our mixed air condition would be a product of very cold outside air and building air returning to the unit. Perhaps some preheating would be required to raise the mixed temperature to 60°. The addition of heat, while raising the temperature, will lower the relative humidity, resulting in fairly "dry" air. If space reheat coils are utilized for final thermal conditioning, this will cause low humidity problems in the conditioned spaces, evidenced by discharges of static electricity when people walk across the rug and touch metal objects, and possibly by personal discomfort, as nasal passages dry out. This may call for the addition of a humidifier to our air handler.

Controlling space humidity from a room humidistat, set high enough for comfort but not high enough to cause condensation problems at windows, assures sampling of room conditions where personnel are located, but can be dangerous if not used in conjunction with a high limit, located in the ductwork off the air handler. Allowing the room humidistat to open the humidifier's steam valve, for example, until satisfied, could lead to excessive moisture conditions in the duct, if not checked.

In Figure 45, reverse-acting room humidistat H-1 will increase its pneumatic output on a fall in relative humidity below its setpoint. The reverse-acting, duct high-limit humidistat HL-1 will pass this pneumatic signal so long as its setpoint is not exceeded. Electric-pneumatic relay EP-1 will pass this pneumatic signal whenever the fan is running, and changeover relay CO-1 will pass this pneumatic signal whenever systems are indexed to winter operation. So a normally closed steam humidifier valve can be opened to admit steam to the grid humidifier whenever H-1 needs humidification, provided the foregoing interlocks and safeties are satisfied. Now we have provided for maintaining a minimum relative humidity in the conditioned spaces, with sufficient interlocks and safeties to ensure safe operation: HL-1 does not see excessive moisture in the duct, EP-1 sees the fan running, and CO-1 sees the system indexed for winter.

Our duct himidifier could be an evaporator type, which might use steam, hot water, or electricity as the heat required for evaporation. Or perhaps a water atomizer type would be used, in which water for humidification is atomized to a mist for entrainment in the air stream. But whatever type is selected, these same basic interlocks and safeties could be utilized.

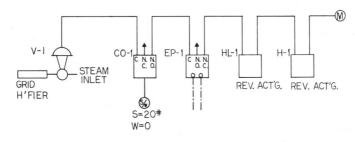

V-1	NORMALLY-CLOSED HUMIDIFIER STEAM VALVE
CO-1	SUMMER-WINTER LOCKOUT RELAY
EP-1	ELECTRIC-PNEUMATIC RELAY WIRED TO FAN STARTER
HL-1	HIGH-LIMIT HUMIDISTAT MOUNTED IN DUCT SAMPLING BOX.
H-1	ROOM HUMIDISTAT

Figure 45   Space humidity control.

INTERLOCKS AND SAFETIES

Before leaving controls for air handlers, we need to examine interlocks frequently called for in air handler control work and also to look at safeties used in conjunction with fan control.

Large fan systems when started often initiate start-up of associated pieces of equipment, designed to run at the same time as the fan in the air handler. Typical pieces of equipment often specified to be interlocked with the air handler supply fan are (1) the system return fan, (2) coil pumps, (3) space exhaust fans, (4) air handler electrostatic filters, or dry filter media advance mechanisms, and (5) chillers, designed to serve only the cooling coils of air handlers we might have under control. Remembering Chapter 4 on motor starters, we recognize that holding coil control circuits of the various pieces of equipment starters can be series-wired through auxillary contacts in the supply fan starter, or relays could be used, if the starters were not all in a single motor control center. And it might be desirable to take advantage of low-voltage interlocks of starters that have line voltage coils. Our temperature control panel could be used for control and termination of the various motor control circuits, particularly if it represents a central geographical location in its placement with respect to the various starters under control. Or perhaps the interlocks could be accomplished pneumatically, utilizing EPs and PEs, to minimize conduit and wire requirements. Our sequence of operation on our control drawings should give a description of the startup sequence for future reference by building managers and maintenance personnel. Electric and pneumatic diagrams of the interlocks should be shown, as well, as a part of our temperature control picture.

Safeties will often consist of firestats, smoke detectors, and freezestats. Firestats are temperature-sensitive electric switches, actuated to open their contact on a rise in temperature to their setpoint. They act to stop the air handler supply fan, and associated pieces of equipment, through interlocks, and they require manual reset. Firestat setpoints are generally permitted to be 50° higher than the ambient temperature likely to be normally encountered at their location in the ductwork. Their purpose is to prevent propigation of fire through the building's duct system, by stopping the fans, in the event they sense a high-temperature condition. Manual reset ensures that an investigation will be made, when personnel inspect them, as to why they stopped the fans, rather than permitting the firestat to automatically reset if the temperature should drop.

Smoke detectors, located in the ductwork, are generally wired into the fan circuit, also to stop the fan, to prevent migration of smoke throughout the building, should they pick up the presence of smoke in the ductwork. And usually the smoke detectors will be utilized to annunciate an alarm at the building's fire alarm panel. Smoke detectors perform their task of reacting to the presence of smoke by ionization or light refraction. Ionization detectors make use of a chamber containing a very small amount of radioactive material which will ionize and become conductive to a small pilot current relay whenever the chamber is exposed to products of combustion. This pilot current relay will close its contacts to annunciate an alarm. Light refraction smoke detectors react to smoke obscuration in its photosensitive path, which looks into the duct. Again, a small pilot current relay is activated. Each type utilizes electronic circuitry for amplification of the pilot signal in order to actuate an alarm relay. Multiple contacts may be provided: one to initiate alarm and the other to shut down fan systems. Local fire codes dictate when smoke detectors must be used, usually based on the size of the fan system.

Freezestats are also temperature-actuated switches, whose normally closed contact is wired into the fan control circuit, too. Freezestats will open their contact on a fall in temperature to their setpoint, and manual reset is required. Automatic reset freezestats are available, but their use should be highly selective. Special capillaries, sensitive to the coldest single foot of their length, permit the freezestats to react to isolated cold spots in the airstream, which frequently occur wherever a laminar airflow situation is present. This is an important feature and sets the freezestat apart from the ordinary remote bulb thermostat. It is important that a sufficient number of freezestats be employed, and series wired, to ensure satisfactory coverage of the water coil face area.

7 Terminal Unit Control Applications

As the name implies, terminal space conditioning units are located at the termini of the ducts that serve an area in a building. Control of these units represents final tempering of the conditioned air before it is discharged into the room space. The room thermostat controls the terminal unit. Remembering that section of Chapter 3 that touched on remote conditioning equipment, we shall now look at the controls applied to these various units.

FAN COIL UNITS

These units are not necessarily used at the end of duct runs, although sometimes they do have fresh air ducted to them. Most often, however, they are independent units, designed for either horizontal installation above ceilings or exposed overhead or for vertical installation, either free standing or recessed into wall spaces.

Room thermostats, either wall-mounted or unit-mounted, are used to control the heating or cooling coming from the unit. Let us consider control of a fan coil unit, designed for heating and cooling, and utilizing water as the heating-cooling medium.

In Figure 46, dual-action heating-cooling room thermostat T-1 is indexed for direct action in the winter and for reverse action in the summer, by an intentional change in main-air pressure coming to the thermostat. On a fall in temperature in the winter, valve V-1 modulates open for flow of hot water through the dual-temperature water coil in the unit, and normally closed PE-1 starts the unit's fan motor. A unit-mounted fan switch permits shutting the unit down. The timeclock opens its contact at night to stop the fan. As space temperatures fall to the setting of nightstat NT-1, direct-acting T-1 positions the valve V-1 for full flow

79

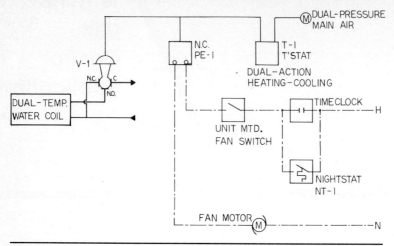

Figure 46   Heating-cooling fan coil unit control with night setback in winter.

through the water coil and allows PE-1 to close, completing the circuit to the fan motor. When nightstat NT-1 makes on a fall in temperature, the unit's fan will be cycled on, until temperatures rise to where NT-1 stops the fan. Next morning, the timeclock closes its contact to run the fan's motor continuously, allowing temperatures to rise to where T-1 will again come into control. On a fall in temperature in the summer, V-1 modulates closed to flow of chilled water through the dual temperature water coil in the unit, and normally closed PE-1 stops the fan's motor. The timeclock opens its contact at night, but space temperatures do not fall, because the unit is shut down, and does not cool, so nightstat NT-1 does not bring on the unit at night.

On a rise in temperature, the above sequences are reversed.

UNIT VENTILATORS

A typical control scheme for a unit ventilator sequences the face and bypass dampers and the ventilation dampers in such a manner that, during the heating season, the fresh air return air damper actuator will begin to stroke, then hesitate, when the coil dampers are positioned for induced room air and for the minimum fresh air mixture to bypass the heating coil. Then the fresh air return air damper actuator would complete its stroke. (The preceding is the sequence on a rise in space temperature at the thermostat.)

These dampers, fresh air, return air, and face and bypass, are built into the unit ventilator and furnished as a part of the unit by the unit ventilator's manufacturer. Very often, they are roll-type dampers, sliding blank off sections designed to revolve when the actuator is stroked. For the fresh air return air, the opening to the fresh air intake would be blanked off as the opening to the return air was opened, proportionately. For the face and bypass, the air access path to the heating coil would be blanked off and the heating coil bypass section would be opened, proportionately.

During the cooling season, when chilled water was being supplied to the coil in the unit ventilator, the fresh air return air damper actuator would be minimum positioned, so that only a predetermined amount of fresh air could be introduced at anytime during the cooling season. This, as in our larger air handlers, is necessary to prevent the introduction of excessive amounts of hot, humid air during the summertime.

We will now look at the controls' layout for such a unit ventilator, designed for heating and cooling, with water as the heating and cooling medium, with provisions for night setback. Let us examine Figure 47.

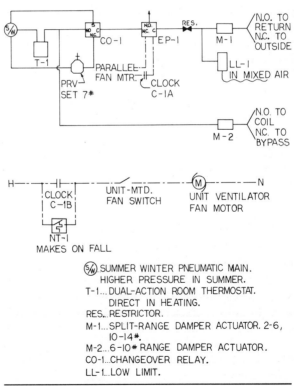

Figure 47   Unit ventilator heating-cooling controls.

When our unit is off, EP-1 exhausts pneumatic signal from M-1, closing off to outside air and opening to return. At night, NT-1 will start the fan on a fall in temperature to its setting, but no outside air will be introduced. No fall in temperature will occur during the night during summer.

When the timeclock closes its contacts for the day operational mode, the fan will start, and EP-1, wired in parallel with the fan motor, will be allowed to be energized, placing M-1 under control.

During daytime during the winter, direct-acting T-1 will, on a rise in temperature, modulate M-1 and M-2 in sequence, according to their spring ranges. This will open the fresh air to a minimum, then bypass the airflow around the heating coil, and then open the fresh air 100 percent except that low limit LL-1 in the mixed air can override T-1 to return the fresh air damper toward the closed position as necessary in order to maintain its 50° setpoint.

During daytime during the summer, reverse-acting T-1 will, on a rise in temperature, modulate M-2. This will open the coil face damper for a greater flow of air across the cooling coil. Changeover relay CO-1 will switch and place pressure reducing valve PRV in control of M-1 to hold it at a minimum position.

In lieu of coil face-and-bypass dampers, a control valve on the coil could just as effectively be used.

Many variations of unit ventilator control schemes are seen, dependent upon whether the unit is heating or cooling, or both, and whether day-night setback is desired. The performance requirements determine the controls to be utilized, and as is the case in most instances, the heating, ventilating, and air-conditioning design engineer will tell us how the unit is to perform. We then select the controls and apply them to make the unit react as required.

UNIT HEATERS

Usually a propeller fan is employed, rather than a centrifugal fan, for creating airflow. This differs from the fan coil units and unit ventilators, where centrifugal fans are used. In unit heater control, the room thermostat can start the fan on a fall in temperature, or operate a control valve as well. If the unit is all electric, the electric resistance heating coil will be energized at the same time the fan is started. A heat dissipation control will keep the fan running for a few moments after the heating coil is deenergized. In unit heaters using gas, the thermostat may open a gas valve, and a plenum thermostat will bring the fan on. When the

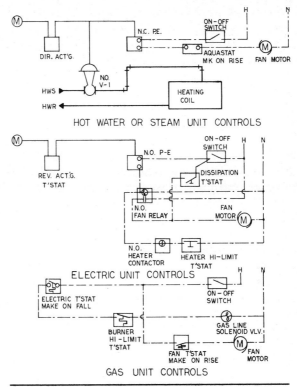

Figure 48   Unit heater controls.

thermostat shuts down the gas burner, the fan continues to run until the plenum thermostat is cooled.

A pneumatic thermostat and PE are frequently used on hot water, steam, and electric unit heaters, but usually, electric thermostats are used on gas unit heaters. The control diagrams in Figure 48 depict basic control schemes for unit heaters.

MIXING BOXES

These terminal units find extensive use in buildings in which temperature control flexibility and system economies are key considerations. Mixing boxes require no wiring, as they make use of the duct static pressure and can throttle down on the cool air flow when the room thermostat is too cool. Single-duct boxes can be fitted with reheat coils for raising their discharge temperatures, should space temperatures continue to fall, while dual-duct boxes can open to the hot deck to blend greater amounts of warm air for space heating. Frequently, the air-conditioning design engineer will select single-duct, cooling-only variable-volume boxes for interior spaces likely to require cooling only, and either single-duct variable volume boxes with reheat or dual-duct mixing boxes for the perimeter areas, likely to require either heating or cooling year-round. Box manufacturers offer a range of sizes so that the designer may select boxes with certain capacities for specific areas. A room thermostat may control one or more of these terminal units, depending on how large an open area is being served. In Figure 49, we see a variable volume box with a reheat control scheme. A falling temperature causes thermostat T-1 to diminish its output. Normally closed air volume damper actuator M-1 returns the volume damper to its minimum position. On a continued temperature fall, control valve V-1 opens for flow of hot water through the reheat coil to raise the temperature of the air being delivered to the spaces, in order to satisfy the demands of T-1. This control scheme may be repeated 100, 200, or more times throughout a building, each area being able to have heating or cooling year-round on a demand basis. Remembering Chapter 6 on air handlers, during cold weather the air handler ventilation cycle will be using outside air for maintenance of discharge temperatures suitable for cooling, while in the summer, the chilled water coil will be supplying the necessary cooling and dehumidification.

A variable volume box without reheat would merely have the reheat coil omitted, and the thermostat would control only the volume damper.

Dual-duct mixing boxes must have both the hot and cold supply ducts run to them, but they do not require the hot water piping that variable volume single-duct reheat boxes require. The central fan may operate at the same speed all the time, because whatever air is refused by the controls in the hot duct will be relieved in the cold duct, both of which are served by the same fan. This gives rise to a need for volume regulation in the box itself, and many dual-duct mixing boxes employ constant volume regulators for this purpose. In Figure 50, we show the pneumatic

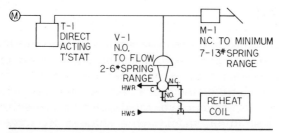

Figure 49   Variable volume box with reheat.

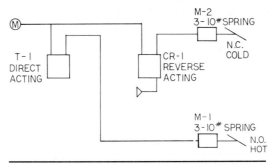

Figure 50   Dual-duct mixing box with pneumatic constant volume.

temperature controls for a dual-duct mixing box with pneumatic constant volume regulation. Note that the thermostat controls the hot duct damper. The volume regulator controls the cold duct damper. As the hot duct damper closes, and volume falls off, constant volume regulator CR-1 opens the cold duct damper to restore the desired volume through the mixing box. This allows each box to seek its own constant volume, in spite of varying static pressures in each of the hot and cold ducts, as different boxes close off to one or the other duct. Should CR-1 introduce too much cool air, thermostat T-1 will react by opening the hot duct damper, causing CR-1 to readjust itself again.

Mixing box manufacturers also offer mechanical constant volume regulating devices that are built in at the mixing box manufacturer's factory, and this eliminates the requirement for CR-1.

As with single-duct boxes, this control scheme may be repeated several hundred times throughout a large building.

Whether single-duct or dual-duct, mixing boxes are a predominant part of the air conditioning system throughout the occupied spaces of many a building.

REHEAT COILS

Whenever duct discharge temperatures may be in need of being boosted in temperature, the reheat coil is likely to be found. Many air conditioning systems in operation today feature reheat coils as the predominant means of temperature control on systems designed to deliver cool air temperatures year-round, suitable for cooling. And often, when areas are served by central station units, under the control of a single thermostat, a remote area close to an outside wall at the end of the duct run may require an additional heat source for occupant comfort during cold

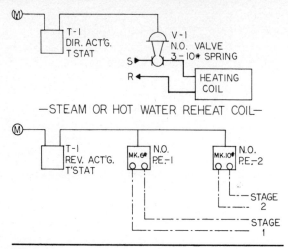

Figure 51   Electric reheat coil.

weather. The reheat coil is nothing more than an in-duct heater, controlled by a thermostat for the purpose of boosting air temperature being discharged into the room whenever the thermostat is too cold. It may utilize hot water, steam, or electricity, and sometimes, gas. Hot water or steam coils require a control valve. This valve, under control of the room thermostat, regulates the flow into the coil located in the air stream in the ductwork. Electric coils may use PEs for one or more stages of control for coil capacity regulation, as in Figure 51, or silicon-controlled rectifiers may vary the intensity of the sine wave for a more evenly proportioned mode of control.

SELF-CONTAINED UNITS

When individual unitary stand-alone operation is desired, self-contained units are often the answer, as they do not require the extension of hot or chilled water lines to serve them, when all electric units are selected. They are readily available as heating and cooling models, utilizing electric resistance heating coils for heat and a hermetic refrigeration system for cooling, or in the case of a heat pump, the hermetic refrigeration system serves both heating and cooling.

These units may be had as through-the-wall models, where the unit is a one piece package, installed so that the condenser coil is exposed to the outside and the evaporator is located inside. In the case of the heat pump, the outside coil affords heat rejection to the outside air when the unit is cooling, but extracts heat from the outside air for use inside when the unit is heating. In practically all cases, unit manufacturers build in all necessary controls, with the possible exception of the room thermostat, so generally there is not much for control personnel to do.

Rooftop units are packaged units designed for installation on the roof, when inside floor space is at a premium, and mechanical equipment may not be allocated space in a mechanical equipment room. Usually, these rooftop units will provide dampers for a ventilation cycle, and pneumatic controls may be chosen by the air conditioning designer to control them, along with the heating and cooling.

Figure 52 is a drawing of a rooftop heating and air conditioning unit. Notice the compactness of the unit, how the essentials are arranged into a single package, which is hoisted and set on the roof over ductwork which has already been roughed to the proper location. The duct is then connected, electrical power is connected, and the controls are connected and mounted. When access doors are in place, the rooftop unit is weathertight, and the air-flow chambers are secured.

Pneumatic lines can come up from below with the electrical conduits, or perhaps could penetrate the roof along with the ductwork. Controls would be installed within the unit and placed according to the requirements for what they are controlling. We shall consider Figure 53 and how it would control this particular rooftop unit.

EP-1 energizes with the fan starter and puts air on the pneumatic controls to place them in operation. On a rise in room temperature, thermostat T-1 deenergizes the electric heating coil through reversing-relay RR-1 and normally open PE-1. On a continuing rise in room temperature, the ventilation dampers will be modulated beyond their mini-

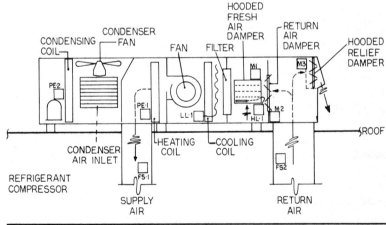

Figure 52   Heating-cooling single-zone rooftop unit.

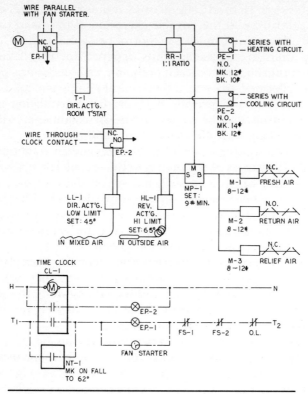

Figure 53   Heating-cooling single-zone rooftop unit control.

mum positions for the introduction of fresh air for cooling, with a proportionate amount of return air being relieved to outside. Should the room temperature continue to rise, the refrigeration circuit will be energized through normally open PE-2.

In the winter, should the mixed air start to fall below 45° during the ventilation cycle, low limit LL-1 will overcall thermostat T-1, returning the ventilation dampers toward their normal positions as necessary in order to maintain its setpoint. In warmer weather, if the outside air rises above 65°, high limit HL-1 will limit introduction of fresh air to the predetermined minimum as set on minimum position switch MP-1, in order to prevent admitting too much fresh air, which is now too warm for free cooling.

When the unit fan is cycled at night in cold weather for maintenance of reduced nighttime temperatures by night thermostat NT-1, EP-2 will prevent any outside air from being introduced into the building, in order to save energy which would otherwise be required to heat this air. Time-clock CL-1 features a manual override feature which allows indexing the building back to day, during that time when the building would otherwise be in the night mode.

Firestat FS-1 and FS-2 will open their contacts to stop the unit should their setpoints be exceeded, as they are wired in series with the overload contact in the unit fan starter.

These controls make heating and cooling on a year-round basis an automatic function of the thermostat, and all the occupants ever have to do is change the temperature on the thermostat, if they like, and override the timeclock at night, should they desire to remain in the area after hours. The clock would automatically return to the unoccupied mode during the next night cycle, if the occupants forgot to return the override lever to night when they left.

In Figure 52, those controls that require a specific location within the unit are identified at their approximate locations. EP-1, EP-2, RR-1, and MP-1 could be located wherever convenient. T-1, CL-1, and NT-1 would be located in the spaces served.

In some cases, arrangements can be made with manufacturers of air conditioning equipment to have them mount controls in the units at the factory. Usually, the controls contractor will pay a mounting charge, but this could be more economical than field installation, particularly if access to certain areas of the unit where controls must be located is difficult.

FINNED TUBE RADIATION

For offsetting "skin" losses in the wintertime, finned tube radiation can be very effective, when placed to counteract the effects of expanses of fenestration often found in extensive use in today's buildings. "Skin loss" is a term applied to the loss of heat that occurs close to outside walls where fenestration or glass is used. By locating finned tube radiation up against the wall under the expanse, we can combat room heat loss by wiping the exterior wall with an upward flow of heat. Application of the heat must be tied to outside air temperature, so that more heat is applied as the differential temperatures increase between outside and inside.

Finned tube radiation is tubing through which hot water is circulated, with vertical fins installed to encourage air flow and to increase heat transfer from the water within to the air flowing across it. You may notice it in enclosures up against the baseboard of outside walls of rooms. Three modes of control are prevalent in commercial buildings: central reset, central reset with local control, or just local control. We shall examine all three to see how the versatility of each of these modes can be used most effectively.

"Central reset" consists of rescheduling the water temperature control point inversely with outside air temperature, similar to rescheduling of air handling unit hot deck and cold deck temperatures, discussed in earlier chapters. But in addition, the effects of "solar loading" must be considered. Consider a large window, with finned tube radiation located under it. On a cold cloudy day, heat loss through this glass to the outside would require heat flow from the finned tube to offset it. But, if the sun comes out, and shines in that same window, even though the outside air temperature is still cold, considerable solar heat is now coming in the window, and we need to throttle back on our finned tube radiation water temperature to compensate for it. So in rescheduling of finned tube radiation (FTR) water temperatures, we apply solar compensators, in addition to our outside air temperature sensors. In Figure 54, we show our controls applied for outside air temperature rescheduling with solar compensation.

Solar compensator SC-1 has the same orientation as the perimeter walls of the zone whose finned tube radiation we are controlling. In this manner, when sun is shining in the windows of the east side of the building, our solar compensator, which is facing east also, senses the load, and lowers the setpoint of our temperature controller. Our solar compensator has a glass window. The containment is ventilated, to pre-

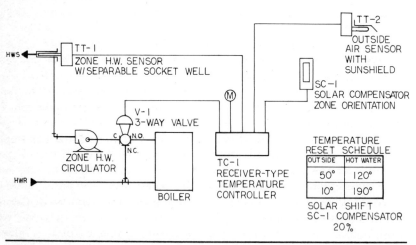

Figure 54   Zone finned tube radiation hot water reset with solar compensation.

vent heat buildup and to assure that only solar load and not trapped containment temperatures affect our compensator. TT-2 is located on the outside of the building with a sunshield, so that it will sense only outside air temperature. TT-1 is placed in the water line going out to our FTR. Water is circulated continuously, below a certain predetermined outside air temperature. From there on, water temperature regulation is the key to proper utilization of our FTR. This particular scheme would be well suited to a large public area, applied to offset heat loss through large glass windows, such as in a hotel lobby, office building reception area, or any such area, which perhaps is served by an air handler, but requires FTR for "skin" loss in cold weather. FTR water temperatures are shown in the reset schedule, but subject to a 20 percent shift whenever SC-1 sees the solar load. Different sides or orientations of the building would be on separate zones to allow for the sun shining on different sides of the building at different times of the day. So different zones of the FTR would be under the influence of SC-1 at different times of the day as the sun made its way from the east side of our building to the south, and then on to the west, later in the day.

SOLAR HEATING

Under control applications, and since we've been talking about solar load, let us now turn our attention to solar heating, in which the energy of the sun is used in place of earth's fuels to generate heat. Orientation continues to be important in solar heating, because our collector depends upon "loading" from the sun in order to collect its energy.

Pneumatic temperature controls can play an important part in any solar heating project, perhaps more appropriately called "solar energy project," because there is a need to regulate collector input to our system being served, and also to divert the collected input to storage for use when the sun is not shining. Diversion for storage can take place whenever immediate system demands are satisfied, because collector activity continues all the while the sun's energy is predominant in our area.

Collectors must present maximum surface area for exposure to the sun's rays. So the plate type collector is perhaps the most widely used type at this time. It generally consists of a nonreflective, heat absorbing surface through which a liquid medium is piped and circulated. Good thermal conduction is important, so nonferrous metals such as copper or aluminum can be used quite effectively when painted black. A glass covering helps to lock in thermal action and prevent dissipation by the cooling effects of outdoor air temperatures or wind.

91

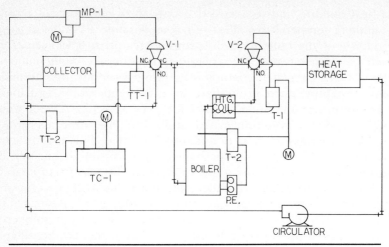

Figure 55   Wintertime heating with solar generation controls.

In Figure 55, we have made provisions for collector discharge temperature control, important to the prevention of reverse action in our piping system, as well as diversion temperature controls, which react to divert collector energy output to storage upon sensing that immediate system needs are satisfied. Continuous flow provides for heat reclamation from our storage source when collector activity is down, and there are supplemental heat source controls for those periods when "free energy" supplies are dwindling.

Temperature controller TC-1, which is direct-acting, will, on a fall in temperature at TT-1, modulate three-way control valve V-1 to bypass water around the collectors. Minimum position switch MP-1 permits establishing a minimum water flow through the collectors of 2 percent, to ensure that TT-1 can sense collector activity, when it resumes. On a rise in temperature at TT-1, TC-1 will modulate V-1 for up to full flow through the collectors, as long as collector discharge temperature stays above TT-1. Collector return water sensor TT-2 resets TC-1 upward as returning water temperature rises, to make sure that the temperature of the collectors is always higher than the return.

Heating coil remote bulb thermostat T-1 modulates three-way control valve V-2 to bypass water around the supplemental boiler and heating coil, as discharge air temperature rises above its setpoint. In this manner, collector hot water is sent to storage and ensures that the supplemental boiler heats water when necessary for the heating coil only. Boiler water discharge thermostat T-2 energizes the boiler through PE when necessary for supplemental heat input.

When collector activity is down, hot water from our storage source is utilized as long as it has enough heat to satisfy T-1. Should reserves be exhausted, T-2 will energize the boiler to maintain hot water for heating.

The system circulator may be started automatically from outdoor air temperature or started manually, as need requires.

8 Temperature Control Accessories

WELLS

Thermostats, sensors, and controllers, designed to be used for water temperatures, can be installed so that the instrument, when removed for servicing or replacement, does not require draining the system to prevent the escape of water. The sensing bulb of the instrument will be inserted into a separable socket-type well, which is permanently installed into the piping system or vessel. The well, usually manufactured of copper, is inserted through a threaded fitting and protrudes into the water. It is closed on the submerged end, and when screwed into place, prohibits leakage, while offering to the sensing bulb an environment totally surrounded by water.

Wells come in varying lengths, to suit the sensing elements for which they are designed. Their installation is frequently through an end of a tee, or through a welded, threaded fitting in the heel of an elbow. When pipe size permits, they may be installed into the side of a pipeline, but only where the well is sufficiently short and stout to sustain turbulence. General practice and recommended procedure is to install the well angled in the direction of flow. This permits the well to be of minimal resistance to waterflow, minimizes turbulence, and assures trouble-free performance (see Figure 56).

The well is appropriately named, because it represents a depression into the water and extends to a depth of from 5 to 15 in., depending on the requirements of the instrument being used. Most manufacturers' wells require 1/2- or 3/4-in. threads on the fittings in which the installation of the well is intended. Where larger openings are encountered, bushings can be used to reduce the size of the tap to that required for installation of the well.

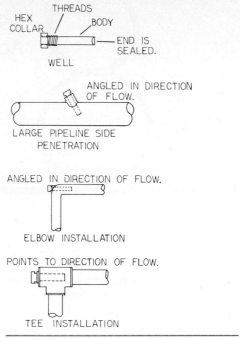

Figure 56   Thermal well and its installation.

When high temperatures or corrosive conditions are encountered, wells made of stainless steel are used and are available made of other materials, as well, to suit many varied applications.

The bulb of the instrument, when inserted into the well, will sometimes be installed with conductive gel first injected into the well to improve heat transfer and assure maximum responsiveness and bulb sensitivity. The bulb can be removed anytime, but the well becomes a permanent part of the piping system. So complete freedom of removal is provided for the pipeline controller, sensor, or thermostat. And, protection of the sensing bulb is provided, as well.

SUNSHIELDS

Remembering our earlier discussion concerning chilled water and fresh air changeover, we recognize a need for our changeover thermostat to sense the temperature of the outside air. The desired location is generally the shaded side of the building, away from the rays of the sun. But many buildings are subjected to direct sunshine on all sides at least once during the day, and we may not have a convenient fresh air intake duct, offering a louver behind which we can mount the thermostat bulb.

When the bulbs must be installed on outside walls, they must be protected from the influence of the sun, because we are interested in heating-cooling decisions made on the basis of outdoor air temperature, rather than temporary high temperature influences of the sun. So a sunshield is used to protect our thermostat bulb from these rays. Angling over the bulb like an awning, it should be open to free air circulation on sides and bottom. Dark colors on sunshields must be avoided; best are white or silver color for reflectivity. Sometimes sunshields will be inadvertently painted a dark color when other metal trim on a building is repainted, and this creates problems for our thermostat which finds itself too "warm" whenever the sun is shining. The dark color absorbs the heat and falsely influences our controller into thinking "summer" when it still may be "winter." This can result in premature closing of maximum fresh air dampers and unnecessary startups of chillers and associated equipment.

Sunshields come in almost as many different configurations as one can imagine but can be quite simple and be effective. Figure 57 shows a lightweight sheet metal one-piece shield installed on the side of a building, with the thermostat bulb coming through the wall and clipped to the underside of the shield. It should be at a high enough elevation so as not to invite tampering and be positioned away from doorways, which when open, allow warm building air in the winter to rise up to influence the bulb. Also, they should be located clear of shutters, freight docks, or other places which could prove hazardous to them.

GUARDS

The room thermostat, when located in public corridors or high activity areas, will require protection from damage. Gymnasiums are a good example of an area where the room thermostat is susceptible to damage, quite accidental of course, from basketballs and other equipment used.

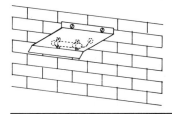

Figure 57   Sunshield.

High volume traffic, frequently experienced in corridors during class changes in schools or during rush hours in transportation depots, can create difficulties for maintenance personnel, who must ensure proper operation of automatic temperature control equipment, because crowding and hurrying causes accidental damage to "protruding" thermostats.

In cases such as this, thermostat guards are provided, to both protect the thermostat from damage and to prevent unauthorized setpoint changes. In "mild risk" areas, the plastic guards with locking covers might be satisfactory, while in "high risk" areas, the heavy metal, concealed access guards would be more suitable. In either case, the guards, while affording safety to the thermostat, are ventilated to ensure proper temperature sensing at the thermostat.

Frequently, in offices or areas where "zoning" has been applied, there may be one thermostat responsible for temperature over a fairly large area. Nuisance setpoint adjusting by occupants who feel better when the thermostat is set as they want it can become severe. Here, a guard is not necessary; the risk is not of thermostat damage but of system setpoint shuffling. So rather than a guard, a concealed adjustment thermostat cover will perhaps be sufficient. This "blank" cover gives no indication of setpoint or of temperature and sometimes goes undetected as a thermostat. But the setpoint is readily adjustable when the cover is removed by special key or wrench by authorized personnel.

A further refinement of the guard is the aspirating box which is installed flush in the wall. The thermostat is installed inside, and room air is aspirated through the recessed chamber, utilizing the Venturi principle. A small amount of control system air is bled through a nozzle within the aspirating box, whose jet is directed toward the "leaving" opening. Room air is induced to flow into the box through the "entering" opening and across the sensing element of the room thermostat mounted inside. Aspirating boxes offer perhaps the best protection for thermostats and humidistats, and they represent the least recognizable appearance.

BULB SUPPORTS

Controllers, thermostats, and sensors used for control of air temperatures will have their elements installed within the ductwork of an air handler. Means must be provided to hold the bulb or averaging element in the correct position. Bulb type instruments will require brackets for support of the sensing bulb, and generally they are designed so that they may be installed from the outside without the necessity for opening the ductwork. Such a bracket is illustrated in Figure 58. Notice that the

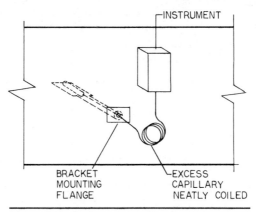

Figure 58   Bulb support bracket.

"body" of the instrument is outside the duct, mounted on the side of it, so that only a hole large enough to permit passage of the bulb itself, and its support, is necessary. "Bend tabs" on the "spoon" of the support secure the bulb to its bed, and the capillary nests in the groove of the bracket. In extremely high velocity or turbulent situations, a piece of tubing may be installed across the width of the duct, and the bulb support bracket is wire-tied or tie-wrapped to it for extra bracing against the heavy air flow.

Averaging elements must be strung or serpentined back and forth to thoroughly traverse the cross-sectional area of the duct in which they are installed to ensure good representative sampling. U-bend or turn-around clips are fixed at opposite sides of the duct, and the averaging element is strung back and forth through them for support and protection. Use of the proper support clips for the averaging element assures that the element won't be bent to too sharp an angle when pulled up snug enough to prevent excessive droop in the cross-sectional spans. Bending the element too sharply will kink it and damage the gas pressure transmission qualities of the capillary. Expansion and contraction of the gas fill within the capillary is necessary to impart mechanical motion at the pressure capsule in the instrument to operate the levers and flexures for regulation of the pneumatic instruments' pneumatic branch line output. In Figure 59, we see the long capillary serpentining the duct area, strung through the u-bend clips on either side. The end may be carefully tied back around itself to form a final ending loop around the last clip.

Care is required in uncoiling long capillaries to prevent kinking or breaking. The tendency is to pull the capillary straight out, but this tightens the twists set into the capillary when it was rolled and packaged. The coils should be carefully unrolled and straightened and gently

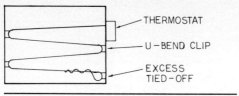

Figure 59   Averaging element strung.

worked back and forth within the unit, to preserve the cross-sectional tubing area of the capillary and to ensure uniform reaction throughout its entire length.

SAMPLING CHAMBERS

Some instrumentation performs better when installed so that its sensing element is exposed to a "sampling" of the controlled medium, rather than being placed in the mainstream. The relatively fragile sensing elements of some humidistats may not perform best if exposed to high velocity air, which could damage it, or impair its accuracy. In these instances, we would utilize a sampling chamber, designed to protect the sensing element, as well as expose it to an authentic sampling of the air stream. Such a sampling chamber could be in the form of a box with preforations in it to admit air, but not at too high a rate, containing a bracket for mounting the humidistat and recessed into the duct, so that its cover plate would be flush with the ductwork. Tubing connection fittings would be built into the box chamber, to facilitate connection of pneumatic piping.

In Figure 60, we show a sampling chamber, in isometric form,

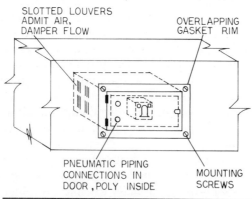

Figure 60   Sampling chamber.

mounted into the side of a duct, with the instrument inside and service-able and accessible from the front through the door which is flush with the side of the duct. The door would probably be gasketed, to help contain duct pressure. The flush rim would best be gasketed, also. A duct sampling chamber such as this would be constructed to fit a specific device, and this device would be capable of being calibrated from the front. Each manufacturer's sampling chamber may vary in configuration, as their controllers do, also. For those manufacturer's whose equipment makes use of common baseplates or frames, the sampling chamber could possibly house a thermostat or a humidistat, or other device, utilizing such a base peculiar to that family of instruments.

In cases of air streams that are contaminated with dust or airborne debris, the sampling chamber would contain a screen or filter, to prevent the entrance of the undesirable matter. This would necessitate frequent inspections and cleaning or replacement to ensure good sampling.

DUCT PRESSURE SAMPLING TUBE

In temperature control work, greater emphasis is being placed upon maintenance of duct pressures, particularly in high pressure systems, utilizing variable volume boxes for control of space temperatures, because savings can be realized in fan energy when fan capacity can be throttled as space temperatures allow it. It is necessary, then, to be able to detect, transmit, and control duct static pressure, velocity pressure, and total pressure. The duct pressure sampling tube is designed for this purpose.

Impact, or velocity pressure is that pressure existing if an airflow in a duct is approached head-on, *minus* the duct static, or bursting pressure. Total pressure is the combination of static and velocity pressure, and static pressure is the bursting pressure being exhibited without the influence of velocity. All three can be measured with the duct pressure sampling tube, which is designed so that it can sense total pressure and static pressure.

Its design consists of a tube within a tube. The outer tube is open through small holes in the side which are presented at a right angle to the air flow. The inner tube is open at its end and is nozzled into the airstream. Each tube offers different tappings on the outside of the duct. Thus a manometer can be connected to read the total pressure or the static pressure; the difference is velocity pressure.

In examining Figure 61, we see the sampling tube installed through the side of a duct to sense pressures inside, with its tappings or pick-up points on the outside, where tubing may be connected, so as to transmit

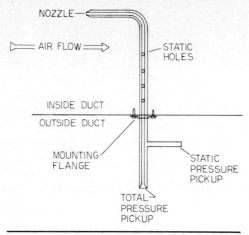

Figure 61   Duct pressure sampling tube.

the signals to a direct-reading instrument or to a transmitter, which may send its signal a hundred feet or more to a remote indicating, recording, or controlling device.

Duct pressure sampling tubes are best installed in a straight run, where turbulence of the air can be expected to be minimized. Different lengths are available to accommodate different width ducts. Multiple sampling can be utilized, with all signals averaged, for good cross representative sampling. A mounting flange or mounting bushing supports the tube and gives rigidity to the tube, so that it might undergo minimum deflection in the face of the oncoming airstream.

Control Wiring

Although we may have basically a pneumatic system, we realize the necessity for electrical wiring as part of our pneumatic system, owing to the EPs, PEs, firestats, freezestats, and other interlocks that might be required. This control wiring is frequently included in the temperature control portion of the work, so a full understanding of the requirements becomes necessary if we are to successfully subcontract this electrical work or have our own electricians perform it.

We shall now consider the electrical wiring requirements for some basic temperature control applications.

Steam or hot water unit heaters will be power-wired under the electrical division of the contract work, but the thermostat and its wiring could very well become the responsibility of the control contractor. In Figure 62, the thermostat breaks the power leg to the unit heater motor so that it can cycle the fan on a fall in temperature. An aquastat is included, to prevent the unit heater from being energized if there is no steam or hot water in the line to the unit. Without this aquastat, our unit heater would blow cold air if energized by the thermostat when no heating medium was available.

Caution needs to be exercised here in the selection of wire size. The electrical division of the job specifications may specify a minimum wire size of No. 12 for branch circuit wiring. In this instance, the branch circuit is actually extended through the thermostat and aquastat before going to the motor, so we would be required to run No. 12 wire and be sure that our devices in the circuit were rated a minimum of 20 amperes. No. 12 wire would be protected back at the distribution panel board at 20 amperes.

The setting and wiring of the manual motor switch and wiring of the unit heater fan motor would be performed under the electrical division. We might very well, then, just run from the motor switch with our con-

103

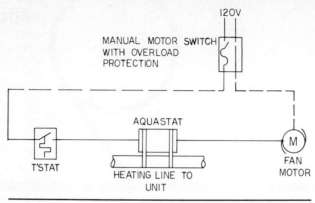

Figure 62 Unit heater control wiring.

duit to the aquastat and thermostat, picking up the circuit just after the contact and overload device in the motor switch, extending it through the thermostat and aquastat and back into the motor switch, where we would make a joint to continue on to the motor. This puts our control devices in series after the switch and overload protection.

Needless to say, local codes governing electrical work would apply, and either we or our electrical subcontractor would permit the job and stand inspection.

When magnetic starters are involved, and we are to connect safeties or other control devices into the motor starter control circuit, we might choose to use No. 14 wire. Frequently the electrical division of the job specifications will permit No. 14 for control wiring. If the motor starter control circuit is derived from an integral control circuit transformer, it would generally be fused, so as to protect the control wiring at a lower amperage, and protect the transformer from overload. Should a remote power source for our motor starter control circuit be required, a spare circuit in a nearby branch circuit panel board might be utilized and protected by a 15-amperes overload device (fuse or circuit breaker). No. 14 wire, then, could be used for our control wiring, as shown in Figure 63.

In this figure, our starter incorporates a control circuit transformer, fused at 2.5 amperes, primarily to protect the transformer. The coil circuit is extended to our safeties, firestat and freezestat, then on to our timeclock (which must be separately powered at 120V), and then on to our override timer, all contacts of which are wired in series, except the manual override, which would parallel the contacts of the timeclock. On the other side of our starter, our EP is wired parallel with the holding coil of the starter through an auxilliary contact in the motor starter.

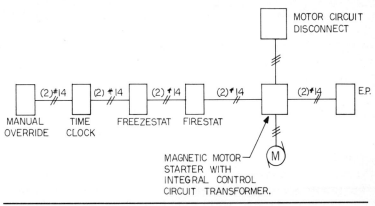

Figure 63   Air handling unit fan control wiring.

Although Figure 63 shows what needs to be done, from a circuiting standpoint, it does not show the work in terms of conduit and wire required, and this is necessary in order to make a determination of how much conduit and wire is required and how much labor is involved. This need, then, leads us to the preparation of a drawing (Figure 64) that can place this work in perspective, or a plan view of the wiring requirements showing routing of the conduit and wire.

Our plan view, Figure 64, shows the work in a form that permits an

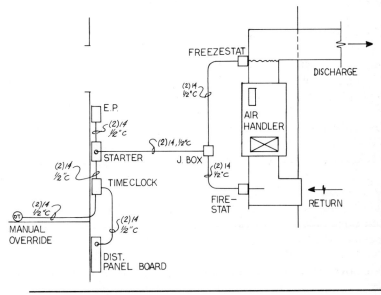

Figure 64   Control wiring, plan view.

electrical takeoff, so that we can estimate it for performance by our own forces, or so that an electrical contractor can estimate it for us. Since it is of no interest to our electrical contractor, no pneumatic work is shown, except that we locate those pneumatic devices which also require an electrical connection.

Our plan view drawing shows our air handler and its starter in an equipment room, with our manual override timer located outside on another wall. This scale drawing and our electrical contractor's familiarity with work within an air-conditioning equipment room, will allow him to properly price this work for us, and it becomes a part of our estimate for a pneumatic temperature control system. Be sure to clarify who mounts the firestat and freezestat. Quite often, our control personnel will mount these, and only wiring will be required of our electrical person. The EP requires pneumatic work, and is mounted by our control technician. The timeclock and override timer will be mounted and wired by our electrical installer.

A layout such as this (see Figure 64) takes the guesswork out of locations for our control devices, and leads to a smoother, less costly installation. Also, when delivered to the building's owner at the end of the job with the control diagrams, it helps him understand the conduit he sees between control devices in his equipment room.

As mentioned in Chapter 5 of this book, locating PEs and EPs to the benefit of the electrician can reduce our wiring costs, and instead give the work to our pneumatic control man. Where only PEs and EPs are involved, a conduit layout might not be necessary, because we are locating our control devices so that they can be connected with a maximum 6-ft piece of flexible conduit, or greenfield. Where this is the case, a count of the devices to be wired with greenfield would suffice.

The use of common conduits can reduce our wiring costs, creating a need for less conduit work between control devices. Consider the following situation. An outdoor air thermostat on the north side of an equipment room starts a boiler on the south side of the room. A thermostat on the south side of the equipment room operates a louver damper on the north side of the room, and a firestat in a duct on the south side of the equipment room is wired into an exhaust fan starter on the north side. These various wires traversing the equipment room can be run in the same conduit, as shown in Figure 65. Each conduit is labeled with a letter (A, B, C, etc.) to aid in identifying its purpose.

Conduit A contains the two wires to the outdoor air thermostat which wires back through D and conduit F to interrupt the boiler control circuit. Conduit B contains two wires to an EP which when energized will switch air to a pneumatic actuator to open the louver damper. These two wires wire back through D and conduit G to the electric thermostat.

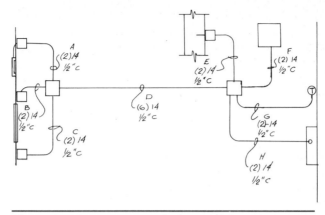

Figure 65   Common control wire conduit.

Power for this circuit is picked up through conduit H, whose two wires go into a local distribution panel board. Conduit C contains two wires which connect the motor starter circuit back through D to conduit E and the firestat in the duct. Thus we have our three, two-wire circuits running through D, which is our common conduit.

Conduit layouts are custom made by the electrical designer in charge of handling the control wiring requirements for the pneumatic temperature control system to ensure that a minimum of conduit work is necessary to accomplish the desired electrical work pertinent to the pneumatic system. They should always reflect a good knowledge of the National Electric Code and local requirements. Frequently, a decision may be in order relevant to whether to substitute pneumatic devices to minimize electrical work requirements, when permitted by specification. We could have utilized a pneumatic outdoor air thermostat and PE located at the boiler, instead of the electric outdoor air thermostat and its associated long wiring runs. And the louver thermostat could have been pneumatic and operated the pneumatic louver actuator directly. But whatever the decision as to the amount of electrical wiring requirements, the layout should be carefully planned so that the best cost estimate can be arrived at, and the work can be clearly defined in terms of how much conduit and wire, and where it goes.

Quite often, electrical metallic tubing is satisfactory for conduit use in commercial buildings, particularly above ceilings, and where not likely to be subjected to physical damage, but, to be sure, check the specifications and local code requirements. If rigid steel conduit is necessary, we need to reflect this on our layout, also, so that this can be taken into consideration during pricing. And check to see whether there are any special requirements concerning boxes and fittings. Stamped steel boxes with knockouts are more economical than cast steel boxes with threaded bosses, and setscrew fittings, when electrical metallic tubing is permissible, could save us money over compression fittings, if they are allowed. Ascertaining what's required ahead of time permits us to prepare an accurate layout and develop price determination based on fact, not guesswork.

The type of wire insulation required can affect our layout, too. Type THHN-THWN is thinner, permitting more wires per conduit size than TW-THW, for instance, but may be more expensive. We need to evaluate the alternatives for the best combination.

10 The Piping System

Pipefitters have historically been the installing trade utilized in performance of pneumatic temperature control work. In the earlier days of this type of work, steel pipe with screwed fittings could be seen in general use. Control devices themselves were larger, heavier, and perhaps less attractive, and an installation took longer to complete. In time, devices became more compact, and tubing replaced pipe. The control panel concept began to dominate many control applications. Let us look, now, at piping systems in general use today.

Before beginning his installation work, the pipefitter-installer should be provided with a piping layout, showing him where tubing is to be run, and how many tubes are required in each run. Control contractors will submit a schematic drawing for approval before installation, and the fitter needs this also, but, for installation use, a construction drawing needs to be prepared for the fitter showing the tubing layout, in riser form or plan view, or perhaps both.

The control contractor's application engineer or planning coordinator will prepare a tubing layout for use in the field. The type of tubing decided upon will be reflected on the construction drawing, also. Materials will be purchased, and delivered to the job site, so that when the fitter arrives to perform the work, he has the plan drawings he needs and the materials with which to perform the work.

COPPER TUBING

Replacing steel piping, copper tubing has come into prevalent use in pneumatic temperature control systems. Soft drawn copper in rolls can be utilized quite well above ceilings, and wherever concealed. Solder or compression fittings allow connections between tubing runs to be made quite easily. Hard drawn tubing finds good application in equipment rooms, where straight runs and turns and offsets made with a bending tool can be made to present a very pleasing appearance.

Instruments installed in equipment rooms can be connected to the copper with compression-to-threaded connectors, or if the instruments feature barbed outlets, the instruments can be mated to the copper with flexible barbed-to-copper adapters. Many of the instruments used in commercial temperature control work today do have barbed ports instead of 1/8-in. female openings, which used to be the rule. This barbed opening is nothing more than 5/32 or 1/4-in. projection (similar to a small nozzle) with a slight raised ring around it, angled back toward the instrument, to facilitate the use of push-on polyethylene tubing for connection. The barbed-to-copper adapter pushes onto the barbed port on one end and slips over the copper tubing on the other.

Copper is especially desirable in equipment areas where high temperatures are likely to be encountered, and when polyethylene under pressure might rupture.

POLYETHYLENE TUBING

Of special importance to the temperature control industry today is polyethylene tubing, made to control manufacturers' specifications, featuring high bursting strength, high melt index, good fire resistant qualities, and exceptional workability. It is used almost exclusively inside control cabinets. And many installations, now, specify polyethylene above lift out, accessible ceilings, and whenever concealed but accessible, it can quite often be run as exposed single lines, provided this installation is neat and professional-looking, with proper supports used at regular intervals. Where the run is exposed, it can be pulled into a raceway system, such as electrical metallic tubing or snap-cover trough. The raceway system for the polyethylene will generally be run to within one foot of the field device, and then the polyethylene can be run that last one foot exposed and then terminated at the instrument.

Also available is polyethylene with aluminum inside reinforcement, which adds rigidity to the tubing but still allows it to be shaped. This aluminum-reinforced polyethylene can be worked with the hands, and although flexible enough to be worked like pure poly, holds its shape like copper.

Multiple tubes inside a factory-fabricated plastic jacket can be ordered, and are especially effective for multitube long runs, because it can be worked as a large, single tube, has good support characteristics, and presents a neat, clean appearance.

Polyethylene tubing is finding increasing use in pneumatic temperature control work today, particularly as control manufacturers go more toward instruments with molded-in barbed type ports. This manufacturing trend has resulted in time savings in the field, as fittings do not have to be installed into the threaded ports of devices that feature these built in barbed ports. It has an excellent history of performance and facilitates modifications and changes to the temperature control system.

TUBING SIZING

Tubes need to be large enough to supply the amount of compressed air required at a stated pressure over a given length. Temperature control contractors have published air consumption figures for their equipment, and these figures coupled with charted pressure drop versus distance figures, allow them to select the right size tubing for any given application. High pressure compressed air, usually in the range of 70 to 90lb, can be piped to strategic locations in large control applications and reduced in pressure locally. This permits the use of smaller sized tubing for exceptionally long runs feeding a remote group of controls than if pressure reduction were to be done at the beginning of the run.

Once the size of the tubes is known, and how many are required, if raceway is to be used, a selection can be made of raceway large enough to hold however many tubes are required. In the raceway layout, pull boxes are spaced every 50 to 80 ft in straight runs, and much closer in runs that have turns and offsets. Tube sizing on large systems is very important. Done improperly, job profits can be lost if replacement becomes necessary owing to lack of air for proper instrument operation. Rough-in of the tubing system is a major part of the temperature control work, so sufficient planning to accomplish the work in an economic manner is necessary to the operation of a successful temperature control office. Sufficient planning, too, will ensure proper operation of the temperature control system to the benefit of the owner of the building.

CONTROL PANEL CONCEPT

Tendencies now are to group control devices within a cabinet. This aids significantly during setup, checkout and even maintenance, by offering at one location the ability to calibrate and initiate temperature control setpoint changes. The sensor-controller system contributed notably to development of grouping of controllers in one location. The temperature control cabinet provides protection for the instruments and affords a degree of security to setpoint manipulation by authorized personnel only. The cabinet concept has had an effect on the requirements for tubing within a fan room, or equipment room, also.

We shall examine the basic difference between the remote controller concept and the control panel concept as it affects tubing routing and controller placement. Let us consider how controls differ for a typical air handler serving remote terminal units and a hot water converter, generating hot water from steam. Figure 66 shows remote controllers and their locations, and subsequently, the routing the tubing would have to take. Figure 67 shows centralized, cabinet-mounted controllers.

Remotely mounted equipment necessitates the installation of main air to five pieces of equipment, in addition to the pneumatic branch lines from device to device. Cabinet mounting facilitates intracabinet piping and requires that main air be run only to the cabinet. Only sensor and branch lines leave the cabinet, and electrical devices can be prewired to terminal strips with numbers to clarify field wiring. Counting one for the

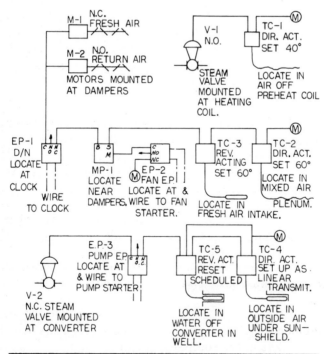

Figure 66   Remote controllers and their locations.

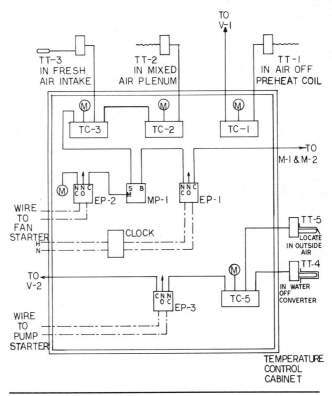

Figure 67   Centralized controllers in cabinet.

main, nine pneumatic lines leave the control cabinet. This could call for the use of a common conduit or raceway, where polyethylene is used, or at least the common grouping of copper lines where they leave the panel. This creates a very pleasing appearance to the installation. As the lines cross the equipment room, one at a time might turn off to go to the instrument it serves. And don't forget, with the sensor lines coming into the cabinet, temperatures can be read out with the use of pneumatic receiver gauges calibrated to match the scale of the sensor-transmitter. The control cabinet approach creates a control center, where the interaction of control devices can be observed. In the remote controller installation, each device must be observed and checked individually at its respective location.

Figure 68, the plan view of the remote controllers, illustrates tubing requirements even better. Consider the layout here that shows the remote controllers in the equipment room.

In the remote controller installation, tubing crosses the fan room

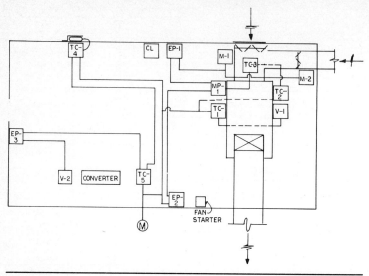

Figure 68   Equipment room tubing layout, remote controllers.

several times, and some piping around the air handling unit itself is required from controller to controller. Figure 69 shows the same fan room, but this time with cabinet-mounted controllers. Control equipment is centralized, and field piping is limited to sensors and actuators.

Raceway with polyethylene or single copper tubes can be used here, and run along together, with a tube breaking away at a strategic point to reach its sensor or actuator. Both methods of controller application would provide the control sequence sought after, but the centralized approach makes for a neater installation. Additionally, the work inside the control cabinet can be performed "on the bench" in the shop. Where several air handlers are to be controlled, this allows a significant part of the control work to be performed in the shop under better working conditions, which should lead to greater efficiency.

The control cabinet approach is pretty much standard today in pneumatic temperature control installations when several controllers are involved. Of course, if the equipment under control requires only a room thermostat sequencing a valve and damper with perhaps a unit-mounted low limit, there might not be the need for a control cabinet. But on a job of any size, there are sure to be controllers and relays required, as we have seen in earlier chapters depicting the application of temperature controls to various pieces of air handling equipment. Realizing that centralizing all control devices may increase the wiring cost of the job, the installation should be carefully studied and well coordinated to obtain the best cost for the most efficient control system

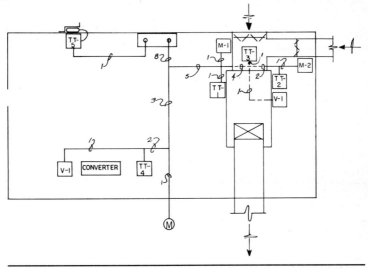

Figure 69   Equipment room tubing layout, cabinet-mounted controllers.

with maximum human-system interface to permit effective observation of control performance and minimize maintenance time required for checking and setting.

Appearance cannot be dismissed from our considerations, either, for the controls contractor wants to be recognized as a quality manufacturer-installer, consistently known for effective control installations that perform well and demonstrate good workmanship.

11 Application Pitfalls

INTAKE-MOUNTED CHANGEOVER CONTROL

Locating an outdoor air temperature sensor in the fresh air intake of an air handler can be an effective means of concealing it from view, so that it doesn't spoil the outside of a building. It's a good location, too, from a functional standpoint. Fresh air being drawn in from the outside is sure to keep the sensor properly aspirated and afford accurate sampling of the outside air temperature. Additionally, a sunshield is not required, because of the sensor's location in the intake plenum, shaded and protected. But caution is to be exercised in selecting the fresh air plenum as the location for the sensor or control. And it has to do with the position of the fresh air damper, and the possibility of isolating the instrument from outside conditions when the damper closes. Consider Figure 70. Temperature sensor T-1 is correctly located. Its position is before the fresh air shut-off damper in terms of air flow. When the unit stops, and the interlocked fresh air damper closes, T-1 will still be exposed to outside air temperatures, migrating in through the continually open louver, whose primary purpose is to prevent the entrance of rain in stormy weather. T-2, on the other hand, will be isolated from the outside air conditions when the fresh air damper closes. T-2, instead, will be trapped within the warmer mixing plenum area of the air handling unit casing or ductwork, and as the temperature around it rises, it may index the systems under its control to "summer." If a boiler interlock is part of "summer-winter" changeover, it may be shutdown and turn off heat to the building. In some cases, chillers may be permitted to start, and their associated chilled water and condenser water pumps placed in operation.

T-1 will be in a position to sample outside air temperatures all of the time, whether the fresh air damper is open or closed. Its sensing bulb

117

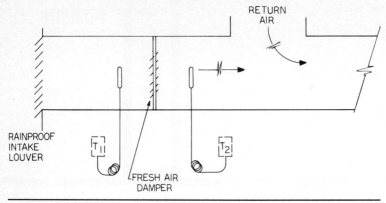

Figure 70   Changeover control location.

could be mounted just far enough inside the louvers to ensure shading, and yet remain essentially in the outside air temperature environment. Locating it before the damper will prevent nuisance changeover when outside air conditions do not warrant it. In large, built-up intake plenums, it may be possible to install the control and its bulb before the fresh air damper is set. In smaller intake plenums, techniques used to mount bulbs in unaccessible areas could be employed, such as the bulb mounting bracket discussed in Chapter 8. In either case, proper positioning of the changeover control or sensor will forestall the premature changeover condition attributable to isolation by the closing of the fresh air damper.

UNGUARDED SENSOR SUNSHIELD

In discussing wall-mounted outside air temperature sensors, we noted the necessity for sunshields to protect the sensor from being tricked by the rays of the sun into thinking that the outside air temperature was warmer than it really was. Premature switching from "heating" to "cooling" is thus prevented from occurring owing to the sun shining on the air temperature sensing element. Care must be exercised in selecting a sunshield so that it does not offer a place for small birds to nest in. Some sunshields, which are open on the bottom, will permit small birds to nest under the shield and around the bulb of our instrument. These sunshields may not employ expanded metal over the bottom. When this happens, mama bird's body temperature is imparted to the sensing bulb, and, here again, the control "thinks" its warmer than it is.

Selecting sunshields that feature expanded metal guards across the bottom, open portion of the shield will prevent the entry of birds seeking a place to nest. Although the bird's selection of the open sunshield is newsworthy and makes an interesting article in the paper when it happens, it could cause problems for the building operator who is concerned about keeping the building indexed for winter, or in seeing that the proper heating hot water temperature is maintained as rescheduled from outdoor air temperature. The type of sunshield becomes almost as important a consideration as the selection of the location for the sunshield.

FIRESTAT IN ELEVATED AMBIENT

It is common practice to select heating control valves to fail-open on loss of air signal. This ensures against excessively cold building conditions should control air be lost for any reason. Frequently, these heating valves on steam or hot water coils of air handlers can cause us a nuisance shut-down problem, if not handled properly on shutdown of the unit. Notice in Figure 71 that firestat FS-1 is positioned to sense the temperature of air off the filters. Heating control valve V-1 is normally open, and the main air to room thermostat T-1 is interlocked to fan operation through EP-1. When the fan is stopped, V-1 opens, and the heating coil is exposed to full flow, causing temperatures within the air handling unit's casing to rise sharply. A normal 125°-firestat will trip out in a situation such as this and will prevent the unit from restarting until FS-1 is reset.

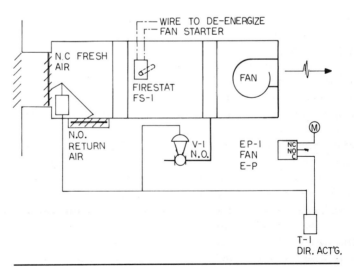

Figure 71   Firestat in possible high ambient on heating and ventilating unit.

But FS-1 will not reset until the casing's temperature is lowered below FS-1's trip point. In such a situation FS-1 would have to be temporarily jumpered out to run the fan to dissipate the heat within the unit to permit resetting FS-1. But imagine the difficulty if the heating and ventilating unit is suspended from a high ceiling in an area where accessibility is quite difficult. Nuisance firestat tripping in that instance would prove to be an extreme difficulty.

One alternative would be to select a firestat whose setpoint was above the high ambient likely to be encountered within the unit at night during shutdown when V-1 failed open. Another might be to install a high limit to assume control of V-1 during down times. Or if local codes permit, perhaps the firestat could be located far enough downstream in terms of airflow from the unit to be unaffected by the high temperatures within the unit at night.

When a firestat is chosen for service in a condition such as we have seen here, caution is to be exemplified in applying the limit control. Consider the firestat's setpoint, and consider the location of the device within the unit. We do want to correctly apply the control for maximum safety in operation of the air handler, but we do not want nuisance tripping to occur, thereby creating hardships for us and the building's operator. And we most certainly do not want to encourage jumpering as a means of getting the fan back on the line for heat dissipation. A jumper unintentionally left in would defeat the purpose of our safety control.

SWITCHING RELAYS ON LENGTHY RUNS

Remembering our discussion in Chapter 5 relative to relays, we shall recall that the changeover or diverting relay responds to an indexing signal to swap ports and switch pneumatic signals to or from a common source. Sometimes a manufacturer will offer a less expensive switching relay which requires a distinct two-position signal in order to affect switching. This can be very much to the customers' advantage if a quantity is involved, as it means savings for them if their application affords a definite two-position mode pressure change as the indexing signal, such as from a two-position pneumatic switch, an EP, or even a two-position pneumatic controller. A need for the slightly more expensive model relay which can react to a modulating indexing signal would not exist, in this case. So the more economical model could be utilized, since we have a distinct on-off type pneumatic indexing pressure.

In applying the distinct mode switching relay, take care not to remote it too far from the changeover signal initiating device. In situations when extensively long indexing runs are necessary, tube capacity coupled with pressure drop transforms the two-position signal into a slowly rising, gradual signal, more modulating in nature than two-position. At the long end of the indexing signal run, it lacks the one-two, definite on-off type punch that was originally intended to be delivered to the switching relay that requires the significantly quick pressure change in order to react.

Reasonable care, and cognizance of the effects of pressure drop, should enable the temperature control designer to avoid this particular pitfall. Small diameter tubing is used more effectively on dead-ended, long, signal type runs. In a 500-ft length of tubing, a gauge at the far end of 1/4-in. tubing would react quicker than a gauge at the far end of 3/8-in. tubing. The larger diameter tubing offers greater volume, which must be filled with air pressure all along the way before we reach peak pressure at the far end. The smaller tube, however, has a smaller capacity to hold air, and less is required to fill it. And on dead-ended runs, where no air will be consumed at the far end, it is preferable to make use of the smaller tubing, which demands less air to fill it and permits quicker response at the far end. This logic appears contrary to capacity tube runs, which feed air to consuming devices. There the emphasis is on sufficient tube diameter to pass CFM requirements, and minimize pressure drop as flow occurs.

In existing installations, where difficulties may already be occurring, the "lagging signal" could be quickened through the use of a volume boosting relay, or receiver controller. In either case, the incoming indexing signal would be amplified by feeding it into our booster device, applying new main, and two-positioning our controller to transmit the changeover signal. Or the switching relay giving trouble can be replaced with one capable of responding to the graduating signal.

FREEZESTAT WITHOUT PREHEAT OR LOW LIMIT

Reflecting on the discussion in Chapter 6 dealing with interlocks and safeties, we remember that the freezestat will open its contact whenever it senses potentially freezing temperatures anywhere along its element length. Located in the mixed air, it prevents the introduction of excessively cold air temperatures onto water coils, which could freeze.

When applied by itself, without benefit of an accompanying pneumatic low limit control, we may find that tripping occurs frequently in cold weather. The low limit, set at, say, 45° will back down on the quantity of outdoor air as required in order to prevent temperature from falling below its setpoint. Usually this would mean reducing fresh air quantities to the preset minimum, but not closing off fresh air completely. Duct airflow design should ensure that return air quantities at that point would deliver a mixed air temperature well above freezestat trippoint, even at wintertime outdoor design conditions.

On air handlers that utilize mixed air temperature controls, they will afford this low limiting feature. But control of fresh air and return air dampers from a space thermostat could be an instance where we might likely see the need for the addition of our mixed air low limit. Also, units that utilize return-air-mounted space temperature controls would need to use the low limit if the return air thermostat was allowed to modulate fresh air.

CONDENSER INTERLOCK

Many air conditioning installations today make use of the "split system," when an outdoor unit containing the refrigeration compressor and air-cooled condensing coils is located remotely from an indoor unit containing the evaporator or cooling coil and inside fan. Refrigeration piping connects the two, and they operate together. Pneumatic temperature controls may start and stop the inside fan, and perhaps modulate a hot water coil valve for heat, and make a circuit through a PE for cooling. Shutdown of the inside air handling part of the split system could be accomplished by a timeclock or handled manually. But an interlock needs to be provided so that whenever the inside unit is stopped, the outside unit needs to be deenergized, also. Failure to do this will result in the compressor continuing to operate, without benefit of the inside fan moving air across the evaporator coil. Lack of airflow will prevent the refrigerant in the evaporator from picking up sufficient heat to maintain head pressure off the compressor, and the outside unit's refrigerant pressure limit control will trip out. If manual reset is required, the outdoor unit will not restart when the indoor section is called upon to operate again. An EP can be utilized effectively to accomplish interlock by wiring it in parallel with the indoor unit fan starter, and piping the signal to the cooling PE through it.

Let's take a look at Figure 72 and note how the compressor interlock with the unit fan is accomplished with the EP. In this case, the PE controlling cooling is located on the roof in the rooftop condensing unit. The signal from the space thermostat passes through the fan EP before being routed up through the roof. A normally open PE is used with a direct-acting space thermostat so a rising space temperature will close the PE contact and energize the refrigerant compressor. But whenever the indoor unit fan is not running, the EP will not be energized and will pass no air to the cooling PE. Further, when the compressor is in operation,

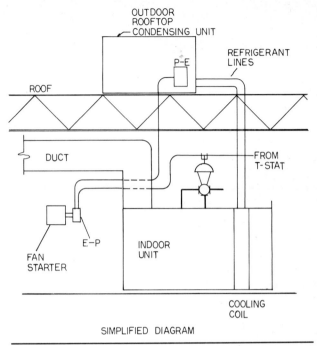

OUTDOOR
ROOFTOP
CONDENSING UNIT

P-E

REFRIGERANT
LINES

ROOF

DUCT

FROM
T-STAT

E-P

FAN
STARTER

INDOOR
UNIT

COOLING
COIL

SIMPLIFIED DIAGRAM

Figure 72   Pneumatic interlock of condensing unit.

stopping the indoor unit will stop the compressor, also, even though the space thermostat may still be calling for cooling.

Failure to route the thermostat's signal through the fan EP would permit the thermostat to energize the refrigerant compressor, even if the indoor unit fan were not running. And this would result in nuisance tripping of the compressor's limit controls, the very thing we want to avoid.

12

Building Automation

INVESTMENT MANAGEMENT

Construction costs for office buildings quite often range into the millions of dollars. Considering this, building owners have the management of a substantial investment on their hands. Developments in the world of temperature controls in recent years have reached toward acknowledging the spiraling costs associated with ownership and management of large structures. The field of temperature controls has brought forth the monitoring and management tools that enable building operators to introduce maximum efficiencies into their operations. These tools are exemplified in building automation systems which frequently are part of the temperature control contract and bear inclusion in this text, since the pneumatic temperature control system is so closely associated with building automation, and since building automation often is specified as a part of the pneumatic temperature control system section of the project specifications.

The theory behind the logic of automation systems is to give better control of the building to its managers. Operating costs make it mandatory that its operators and managers have a good handle on the control of energy consumption through smarter decisions related to maintenance of temperatures, maintenance of equipment, and efficient operation of the building's systems. Why run equipment if it is not needed? Why allow lights to burn if there's no one there? Why maintain comfort conditions at an optimum during unoccupied periods? Why take a chance that routine maintenance, so necessary to the life of equipment, may not be performed? So many decisions similar to these and related to economies in the buildings need to be planned for, recognized, and dealt with. Perhaps it wasn't so critical in years past when energy costs were not so paramount in operational dollar figures. But today it is critical. The mechanical and electrical operations of a building need to be monitored, controlled, and optimized. Today it makes good sense to spend the extra money for building automation because you know your payback is certain. We shall segment our look at building automation systems into three primary parts, identified as monitoring, evaluating, and correcting. As we look at the responsibilities each of these primary parts has to the overall automation management picture, we shall be exposed, too, to the broadly based functional aspect of the system of building automation.

MONITORING

Information retrieval is the base function of the monitoring feature of our building automation system. The need to know what is happening is handled by monitoring devices and data acquisition equipment. Field-installed sensors, similar in purpose to our earlier discussed pneumatic temperature sensors, report to data acquisition equipment in local cabinets strategically installed throughout the building to collect data from the field sensors and to transmit it back to a central processing point command center.

Methods employed in collecting this information have improved over the years. At first, and prior to the time that local data acquisition cabinets were employed, each sensor was wired individually back to a central panel, which may have utilized pilot lights, meters, horns or bells for audible annunciation, and perhaps graphics to depict the basic flow pattern of the system to which various lights or meters related. For example, high discharge temperatures in central station units serving reheat coils or mixing boxes needed to be annunciated to alert maintenance personnel to a failure associated with cooling in that unit, which shortly would manifest itself in high space temperatures, and uncomfortable, complaining occupants. Where several air handlers of this type were under control throughout the building, this meant installing a limit thermostat, and wiring its contacts individually back to the central control panel. If temperature indication was also desired for that same discharge air temperature, a pneumatic transmitter may have been selected for readout on a temperature-calibrated gauge back at the control center, or an electric transmitter could have been used and wired to a common meter on the central panel through selection push buttons for display. In either case, this meant additional wire or tubing run back to our central location. You can see that when several units were involved with three, four, or five similar functions of information retrieval on each one, we quickly generated a handsome quantity of wires and tubing to be installed. Many wires and tubes in large conduits became necessary.

Automation evolution soon produced an improvement to the "hard-wired" concept, where each device had to be individually and permanently wired into the central panel. This next step was the development of a grid wiring system in which wires common to a similar function at various pieces of equipment were connected through remotely operated contacts on a selective basis to first one point, and then another, and the same set of wires carried information from first one and then the other transmitter. Consider our discharge temperature sensor. Each sensor in the discharge of different units was assigned a point number, and by "addressing" that point, we energized a remote relay to connect our sensor wires at that point onto a set of common sensor wires in our trunk cable. When that point was released, another could be indexed or selected, and then the second transmitter's information came in over the same common set of sensor information wires. Our high temperature alarm device's contacts were tied into a common alarm scan initiation circuit, which would cause a central motor driven stepping mechanism to address itself automatically in a sequential fashion to alarm points in the system until it locked in on the point in alarm and acknowledged its report. Thus common wires in an automation cable were extended to data acquisition cabinets, in which selection relays allowed the points to which they were tied to be "online" when so indexed. Common command initiation wires were utilized, also, for starting and stopping of motors, giving us remote control from perhaps one set of "start-stop" switches or buttons at our console. And intercoms at the respective data cabinets could be made to automatically come online when points in that mechanical room were addressed for audible monitoring of equipment startup or shutdown.

Subsequent developments in the area of building automation brought forth information coding equipment for use in data acquisition cabinets that eliminated the need for multiple conductor trunk cables between data acquisition cabinets and the central command point. Manufacturers differ in exact technique employed, but basically both contact closures analogous to limit alarm devices (digital signals) and voltage or milliamp variations analagous to temperature, humidity, or pressure value transmitters (analog signals) can be transmitted over coaxial or triaxial cable, or in some cases, just two wires through discrete coding in units recognizable at the central processor as decodable and reportable values.

Speed is tremendously high today because of the emphasis placed on the necessity to establish high quality, priority reporting of certain critical type alarms. We need to know immediately if a smoke alarm goes off in one of our air handlers.

Rather than attempt to explore the various techniques peculiar to different manufacturers, let us instead consider the performance aspect as might be related to a typical air handler. The automation devices shown in Figure 73 would be separate from and in addition to our pneumatic temperature control equipment, which is required, also, and would continue to go on about its basic business of controlling temperatures.

In Figure 73, automation system sensors are shown located on the air handler and reporting back to data acquisition cabinet DAC-1. Information is daisy-chained through other DACs, until it reaches the central console, where it can be displayed, recorded, or, in a word, evaluated. The smoke detector alarm SDA will close a contact to annunciate the presence of smoke in the return air duct. Mixed air transmitter MAT will continuously monitor and report the temperature of the mixed air. Dirty filter alarm DFA will close a contact to annunciate that the filters are dirty and need changing. Fan bearing temperature transmitter FBT will continuously monitor the temperature of the bearings in the fan to forestall bearing failure, and discharge air transmitter DAT will continuously monitor and report the temperature of the discharge air. All this information is input to DAC-1 and then makes its way back to the central processor console, along with information from other DACs, for owner evaluation.

Auxilliary contacts in starters of fans and air flow switches in ducts can

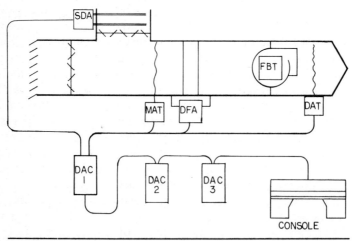

Figure 73   Building automation devices.

tell us when equipment is operating, allowing us to shut it down if it is after hours, and no one is in the building. Current monitors or auxilliary contacts on contactors for lighting circuits can tell us when lights are on in various parts of the building. Temperature transmitters tell us what the temperatures are throughout the building, so decisions can be made related to adjustments upward or downward. And differential type airflow switches report dirty filters that need changing, allowing us to ensure that fresh filter media is in place. Our monitoring equipment maintains a vigilant watch over our building's equipment, helping us to stay out of trouble and operate with maximum efficiency.

EVALUATION

Information thus gathered needs to be acted upon to derive benefits from the monitoring process. The processor and associated human-machine interface console or operator's terminal allows us to input certain parameters relevant to system limits and control points. Computer-based automation systems permit volume information storage and mode modification through operators' terminal keyboards, allowing us to "tell" the machine what to look for and what to do when certain conditions arise. Consider our smoke detector alarm (SDA). Our processor may be instructed that a normal condition is the absence of a contact closure. Upon receiving a signal from the SDA, an evaluation occurs in which the machine sees an abnormal situation. In the absence of programmed information, we might have an operator on duty full time, instructed to recognize an alarm point at SDA as a priority condition, requiring immediate reaction. A mixed air transmitter will be allowed to input information within preestablished limits. Should they be exceeded on either end, our automation processor's evaluation can be programmed to recognize it as an alarm condition. Dirty filter alarm DFA's contact closure will be recognized as a maintenance alarm, not assigned the priority of our SDA. The fan bearing temperature transmitter's information would be assigned a high limit, and an alarm evaluation process would result in recognition by our processor as a high level maintenance alarm. The same could be true for discharge air transmitter DAT. The evaluation process thus undertaken by our processor or by our full time attendant will result in decision making related to reactions designed to acknowledge and correct. The evaluation utilizes primarily centrally based processing equipment in handling information from our field sensors. This is in contrast to the monitoring segment of our automation picture, which utilizes primarily field-installed devices out "where the action is."

CORRECTING

Reaction to information input takes the form of command initiation. Centrally based equipment instructs field-mounted actuators to respond. The same information input path is used to transmit commands back to the field through our DACs. Consider the alarm coming in from SDA. The system is set up to sound an alarm through the building's fire alarm system and to position smoke dampers for containment and purging. An alarm contact in one of our remote DACs may close to initiate alarms throughout the building via the building's fire alarm system. Additionally, EPs will be energized to apply main air to selected damper actuators to close floor smoke dampers and to open air handler unit fresh air and exhaust air dampers while closing the return air damper. So when the alarm is being turned in, the air handler sets itself to rid the area of smoke to enhance the chances for survival of people possibly still on the floor.

Our mixed air transmitter offers temperature information at any moment which can be displayed at our command center, or logged perhaps through a printer. Should temperature drop sharply or rise sharply beyond our preestablished limits, this would be displayed and recorded at our console at the moment it occurred. Possibly instructions could be printed out to dispatch maintenance personnel to the air handler for investigation. If an outside air damper had stuck open for any reason with the attendant risk of coil freezeup in extremely cold weather, damaging consequences might be circumvented through timely alarming and investigation.

The dirty filter alarm DFA correction action might take the form of startup of the automatic filter drive mechanism to advance the dirty medium out of the way and pull in a new medium from an automatic feed roll. By limiting the run time of our filter drive mechanism through a timer, we can run the advance drive unit just long enough to ensure a clean medium from top to bottom. When the clean medium is in place, our DFA will return to its normal state. At our console, the times of the alarm, corrective action, and alarm clearing could be logged. In the event the medium runs out, the DFA would stay in alarm until maintenance personnel replaced the medium roll.

The fan bearing temperature transmitter might be tied into the fan starter's circuit through alarm-initiated relays to stop the fan in the event high bearing temperatures are encountered. Additionally, audible alarming at the console and logging of the time of the bearing temperature alarm would call for immediate attention from maintenance personnel.

Discharge air temperature limits would be selected to permit fluctuations within a permissible span. Beyond those, an alarm condition existing in the discharge air might signal failure of the cooling system, if temperatures were too high. Corrective action might take the form of merely audible alarming to draw attention to the fact that no cooling was now being delivered by this unit.

We see in our building automation system the closed loop of monitoring, evaluation, and correction. Many more alarm and monitoring functions are prevalent, and only these few were selected to demonstrate the way in which an automation system can be used to the benefit of the building's management team and its occupants. Maintenance alarms alert personnel to required services to prevent equipment failure. High level maintenance alarms call on them to inspect for unsatisfactory temperature fluctuations. And critical alarms tie in with building life-support systems designed to make our buildings of today as safe as possible. And automatic response by our central equipment ensures setpoint modifications and equipment startups and shutdowns that correspond with the more economical schedules permissible with energy saving programs designed to hold down excessive operation of HVAC equipment.

13

Checkout
and
Calibration

After installation of a control system is complete, the next steps have to do with commissioning the system or startup. Placing the controls into operation centers around checkout of the devices as to whether they are properly connected and installed to perform as intended and calibration of the devices so that their response occurs at the level of variation intended in the medium under control. Each device should be checked out, but each device may not require calibration. Many are factory set or factory-calibrated. Room thermostats, for example, are usually factory-calibrated and can be installed and placed into operation by operation of the temperature setpoint lever to see if branch pressure buildup and bleeddown occurs at approximately room temperature when the setpoint lever passes the corresponding setting on the thermostat's dial or scaleplate. Firestats may be factory set at 135°. Checkout might consist of manually tripping the firestat to be certain that it does shutdown the fan or perform the intended function. We shall examine the activities of the checkout and calibration people as they concentrate on various control devices within the control system. We shall "follow them around" as they approach each of the control devices, and we shall discuss the activity they might go through in their process of checkout and calibration of the pneumatic system of temperature control.

ROOM THERMOSTATS

Assuming there was no air in the system when thermostats were mounted, our checkout person will go to each one and check the thermostat's branch pressure output in response to setpoint dial movement. Thermostats will generally feature a branch line tap port which permits the insertion of a small pressure gauge using a special fitting. In this way

133

the pressure response in the branch line can be observed while the set-point is being "swung." If the room thermostat controls a reheat valve, stroking of the valve will be observed while the branch line pressure is increased and decreased. The branch line pressure buildup and bleed-down should occur within a predetermined temperature change range. If the throttling range or sensitivity of the thermostat is 4°, our checkout person will be sure that the 4° swing produces the 3- to 15-lb pressure change desired. Then the thermostat will be set at the temperature shown on the control manufacturer's shop drawings, and the cover will be reinstalled.

FIRESTATS, FREEZESTATS, AND SMOKE DETECTORS

These devices, and any other safety devices wired into the fan circuit and designed to stop the fan if their setpoints are reached, are checked by tripping each one to be sure fan shutdown occurs. Sampling tubes for duct-mounted smoke detectors, if such are used, must be checked for proper positioning in the ductwork to enable sampling to take place through the sensitized portion of the detector. Firestats and freezestats, if not factory set, should be adjusted to setpoints reflected on the shop drawings.

AIR HANDLER SENSORS AND THERMOSTATS

Installation of the sensor or thermostat at the proper location on the unit or in the duct work needs to be verified. Sensor-transmitter output pressure should be read and compared with a temperature-pressure chart which lists what the pressure output should be at any given temperature. A test thermometer can be inserted at the same place as the sensor for the actual temperature reading. Gauges are available which are multirange-calibrated over a range of 3 to 15lb. These multiranges are in degrees, and when the temperature range of the sensor-transmitter is known, the corresponding gauge range can be observed to see whether output matches a test thermometer. Some few sensor-transmitters may include calibration screws or other adjustment means to permit range alignment if some deviation is noted. Most sensor-transmitters are factory-calibrated only, often meaning that replacement is encouraged rather than adjustment. Thermostats or controllers with self-contained bulbs and capillaries need calibrating. This consists basically of adjusting the device for branch pressure equilibrium when controller setpoint is lined up with actual temperature ambient at the sensing bulb. Prior to this, throttling range is adjusted and checked. Then the duct temperature is taken, and the setpoint is adjusted to correspond with the actual termperature. Then a calibration screw or adjustment knob is turned until branch pressure output equals the midrange point of the device under control. After that, the setpoint is adjusted to that desired. The device is then said to be in calibration, or ready to respond with corrective action when temperatures approach its setpoint.

If the device under control is a valve or damper actuator with a spring range of 8 to 13lb, the midrange point of the device under control would be 10.5lb. If two valves were sequenced, with one having a spring range of 2 to 7lb, while the other had a range of 8 to 13lb, then the midrange point of the devices under control would be 7.5lb. The idea here is that the output from the control should be equal to the midrange of the responding actuators when the temperature under control equals the setpoint of the controller.

RELAYS, EPs, AND PEs

Pneumatic relays, solenoid air valves and pressure switches must be examined individually to determine if the correct piping and wiring has been accomplished. Hand actuated squeeze bulbs are a valuable tool to the checkout person, because switching relays can be pumped to their respective switchover pressures and observed for proper operation. PEs can be pumped and their contact closure observed. Should deviation from the desired make-break point be the case, pressure adjustments in the PE permit raising or lowering its reaction point. One should check for correct wiring terminations. Frequently single-pole double-throw switches are incorporated in the PE, and this generally leaves one pole unwired. Verify that the correct two are wired into the circuit under control. Solenoid air valves or electric-pneumatic relays (EPs) should be energized and their output noted. EPs can be piped so as to pass air or to bleed air when energized. Check job drawings and make certain the EP is piped correctly. Ascertain whether the correct voltage coil is incorporated into the EP. Sometimes the controls designer assumes a 120-V coil in the motor starter and specifies that the EP be wired parallel with the coil in the starter. If the starter utilizes 208V or 240V for the control circuit, the coil in the EP may have to be changed. Activate the control system and observe signals from other pneumatic relays to check their operation.

CONTROL VALVES

Watch for piping errors related to control valves. If a two-way straight through control valve is piped in backwards, it must be turned around so that its seat moves toward closeoff against the flow in the pipeline. Three-way control valves are frequently piped incorrectly, if inadequate supervision was present when the valve was installed. Three-way valves designed for mixing service must not be installed in diverting service. You will remember from the discussion in Chapter 5 concerning three-way valve design that the seat in a mixing valve will become severely unbalanced if the valve is piped for diverting service, resulting in poor control, pipeline noise, and damage to the valve.

Apply signal to the valve actuators and determine that the valve closes properly. This is best done when pumps are on and water is flowing in the piping system. Then problems related to flow can be identified, if they exist. The valve should have the ability to open and close smoothly against system pressures. For control valves serving water coils in air handling units, see that temperature change occurs in the air off the coil when the valve is stroked, and the air handler unit's fan is running. Also verify that the stroking of the valve occurs over the spring range as specified on the drawings. This will ensure that the correct spring is installed in the valve actuator. Valve actuators should be over the top of the control valve. A valve lying on its side will permit water system grit to accumulate around the valve stem, and premature wear of the stem seals will occur. Observe that no leakage occurs from the valve stem, which could indicate poor seals or a loose packing nut. Sufficient space should be provided, also, to permit removal of the actuator and valve stem for future service and maintenance of the control valve.

DAMPERS AND ACTUATORS

Control manufacturers' guidelines provide means for the controls application engineer to determine the number of damper actuators required for any specific damper, based on damper size and system static against which it is to operate. So the correct number or size of actuators should have been shipped to the job and installed by our fitters when they put the job in. But if the dampers were provided by others, and quality control dampers were not furnished by the controls contractor, the torque requirements may be different than those planned on, or assumed. Apply signal to the actuators, and see that dampers rotate smoothly, and without hesitation. If the actuators utilize positioners, set them for the desired movement when proper signal is applied.

Closeoff is extremely important, particularly on outside air dampers, to protect against migration of freezing air temperatures in the wintertime into the air handling unit. Linkage adjustment allows us to set the dampers so that closeoff occurs just slightly before the actuator spring returns to its normal position. This places spring tension on the fresh air damper to hold it tightly closed when the fresh air damper actuator positions it for closeoff.

If dampers are to be sequenced with other control devices, put the system through its paces and see whether the desired sequence occurs. Set positive-positioning devices if they are used. Make sure the dampers are installed squarely, and if not, bring this to the attention of the installing contractor, usually the sheet metal and ductwork contractor. If the weather is cold, take readings in the mixed air of the air handler as the dampers modulate, to determine whether stratification may become a problem. Be in a position to recommend baffling or turbulators, if required. Work with the balancing contractor to set the minimum outside air damper position control, if need arises.

RECEIVER CONTROLLERS

One-input, two-input, or three-input controllers may be utilized on the job. The one-input model has to do with the one incoming signal from the temperature transmitter sensing the pressure, air or water temperature to be controlled. Two-input speaks of the second signal applied to reset controllers, when primary temperatures are rescheduled from the signal from a secondary transmitter. And three-input indicates remote manual reset from a modulating signal pneumatic switch, or scale shift reset from a third transmitter. Calibration is necessary and usually consists of the following elements: (1) setting the throttling range; that is, determining how many degrees change we shall permit in order to affect a branch line pressure change off our controller from 3 to 15 lb; (2) setting rescheduled setpoint into the controller, or determining what primary temperature is to be called for at various input levels from our secondary transmitter; (3) adjusting the controller for equilibrium, when adjacent scale values are introduced into the primary and secondary ports; that is, getting actuator midrange pressure in the branch line of the controller when pressures, corresponding to desired primary transmitter signal pressure at a given secondary transmitter signal pressure, are applied to the appropriate transmitter input ports; (4) setting scaleplate so that desired control point without reset lines up under setpoint indicator, and noting reset scheduled into the receiver controller somewhere on or around the device, or under its cover; and (5) applying the third scale shift pressure to see that the desired elevation of setpoint occurs when this override pressure is introduced into the controller. Variations in this procedure may exist from one manufacturer to the other, but the basics discussed above will generally hold up for any of the steps encountered. This calibrates the receiver controller. We commission the instrument by reconnecting the sensor lines and the branch line to the actuated device under control.

TIMECLOCKS, OVERRIDES, AND NIGHTSTATS

Nighttime shutdown and lowered setpoint temperature control of our air handlers needs to be checked. The building manager or owner can tell us what startup and shutdown times for which to program the timeclock. Trip the clock to be sure that shutdown of the unit occurs. Then operate the manual overrides and night thermostat to see that they can restore unit operation. Set the temperature adjustment on the night thermostat to match shop drawing requirements, or as directed by the owner. In night setback systems employing removal of main from a pneumatic night thermostat during the day for fan continuous operation, check the setting of the PE to be sure contacts are opening and closing. Instruct the owners or occupants that the night thermostat cannot affect daytime temperature changes, and explain that it is there for nighttime control only.

DUCT PRESSURE CONTROLS

Setup of these devices is to be approached carefully. If fans are running on large, high pressure systems, cycling of fan capacity actuators can cause duct damage. During checkout and calibration, it may be advisable to begin with open mixing plenum access doors to lessen the chance of excessive negative pressures, only until the controllers are recognized as being setup enough to maintain control. Adjust transmitters for precise signal output and then controllers for accurate reaction. Use quality static measurement instruments, and compare readings taken with readings received at the controllers. Coordinate your checkout and calibration activities here with the fan's manufacturer, who generally supplies supervisory personnel during startup of the equipment.

14

Maintenance Tips

Good performance that spans the years must be tied to an effective maintenance program that serves to keep your pneumatic temperature control system in peak operational form. Control manufacturers offer contractural maintenance services, and this is good insurance against malfunctions and inefficiencies that can arise in aging, unattended systems. Clean, dry air is essential to your pneumatic system. It was clean and dry when it was installed, and it must be kept this way. Proper intake and discharge filtering at the compressor must be preserved, as well as dehumidification of the compressed air. Good controls deserve good compressed air, and the owner reaps the rewards when emphasis is placed on proper maintenance. Damper actuated linkages should always operate smoothly, and certain strategic lubrication points should be periodically attended to. Control valves need to close off properly and must not permit leak through when controllers say "close." Let us now take a look at our pneumatic temperature control system with an eye toward proper maintenance and things to look for and be aware of during our system inspections.

AIR SOURCE

The air compressor is the heart of the pneumatic system. For many years, it will be expected to provide the proper quantity and pressure of compressed air to our controllers. Examine it periodically to ensure that it remains properly equipped to do its job. As it operates, air is drawn in for compression and delivery to the storage tank. In the intake is a filter to trap dust, dirt, and airborne grit, that would otherwise find its way into the air system. This filter is replaceable, and when it becomes dirty and is

139

no longer able to perform its task, replace it. Remove the medium and inspect it to see when that time has arrived.

Piston compressors are lubricated by oil in the base of the pump unit. Generally, a dipstick or other means of level measuring are provided. This oil level must be maintained at the appropriate point. Too little oil may lead toward "dry" operation of the pump unit and subsequent damage. Too much oil can result in air contamination, as overfilling encourages the pump unit to discharge oil or oil vapor into the storage tank. Be sure the right level is maintained. It is usually quite easy to check, and maintenance of the proper oil level is a very basic function. Follow manufacturers' recommendations relating to type of oil to use and frequency of changes.

Your air compressor was sized by the control manufacturer to operate with sufficiently long off periods to ensure motor and pump cooldown between pumping cycles. If you notice excessive compressor on-time, this could be an indication of a leak somewhere in the system. Through sectional isolation of the piping system, and subsequent observation of compressor run-time, the trouble can be pinpointed. Permitting the compressor to run excessively contributes to premature wear and necessitates more frequent maintenance functions. Additionally, a motor operating under long load cycles may cause motor overcurrent protective devices in the starter to trip at a time when personnel are off duty. If the sizing of the overload sensitive units was marginal, nuisance tripping may never evidence itself until compressor "on" cycles are substantially lengthened.

Good practice calls for installation of a tank drain on the compressor's storage tank to remove accumulated moisture, as a result of compression of the intake air which results in the moisture being "squeezed" out. However, if project specifications did not specifically call for one, it may have been omitted, and in this case manual draining of the tank at regular intervals is required. This water, which is separated from the compressed air under compression, never finds its way to the dehumidifier for removal, because it remains in the bottom of the tank. If not drained, it begins to occupy space in the storage vessel reserved for air. This diminishes the tank's capacity and shortens compressor "on" and "off" cycles, thereby increasing the number of starts per hour. Increased wear on starter, motor, and pump is the result. A continued buildup will result in water being pumped into the system, as the water level reaches the tank's discharge point. Needless to say, the dehumidifier would not handle that load, as it was not sized to condense flowing water from the system, only moisture entrained in the air. Drain the tank weekly, if an automatic drain was not provided, or spend the small sum necessary to have one installed.

Make it a point to routinely observe tank air pressure. The cut in and cut out points of the pressure switch should remain constant, and switch action should be a definite, two-position reaction. If vibration exists at the unit, either from poor mounts or the loosening of components, "contact bounce" may occur, as the switch reaches the cut out point, and starter "chatter" may be observed just prior to unit shutdown. Unchecked, this will result in starter damage, and eventually the compressor will not run. Contact bounce can be seen in older units, in which vibration is a problem, and after aging has affected the off center spring in the pressure switch. Secure the compressor properly, if it has worked loose. Tighten components and replace the pressure switch, if suspicious.

Dehydration of the compressed air is accomplished as the high pressure air leaves the storage tank. Lowering the temperature of high pressure air condenses more moisture than low pressure air cooled to the same point. A temperature-pressure relationship exists in condensible gases that says the greater the pressure the higher the temperature at which the gas in question will give up its moisture. Our dehumidifier or dryer, as it is popularly called, cools the high pressure air as it passes through a refrigerated chamber and causes moisture entrained in the air to condense. Subsequently, the moisture is trapped and dumped to the drain. This ensures that the air, as it makes its way to our controls in the system, will not give up any moisture in the piping system, and that no moisture will appear in our control devices to hamper their operation.

If your dryer has an alarm light, visual notification will be given at the dryer whenever the chamber's temperature is above a predetermined "safe" limit. In lieu of this light, chamber temperature may be taken on some units with a test thermometer. It should range between 35 and 38°. The piping leaving the dryer should be quite cold to the touch. Be sure the trap in the dryer remains active and does not hang up because of fouling at the dump valve from accumulating sludge. Take particular note that the water level does not rise beyond half way up the bowl of the trap.

The final filter is next in line, as the air makes its way to the system. Keep it clean. Replace the filter medium, when dirty, and if moisture is seen to be accumulating in the filter's bowl, suspect the dryer and its trap.

Finally, the pressure reducing valve should be checked to ensure constant system pressures as required by the installation. Many incorporate a locknut to permit locking the setting. See that this is secure after making any necessary setting adjustments. Gauges on both sides of the pressure reducing valve (PRV) will enable you to see how the PRV is performing.

Relief valves are installed on the compressor and on the low pressure line, after the PRV. Periodically pull the check ring to raise the pin and allow them to blow momentarily. This ensures free spring action and an open port to the atmosphere whenever they are required to vent. The one on the compressor protects the tank from overpressure, and the one after the PRV protects the system's controls from overpressure.

And watch for worn belts and improper belt tension between the electric motor and the pumping unit. Normal deflection for belts may be in the range of 1/2 to 1 in., when depressed with the finger. (Be sure the disconnect is pulled on the unit when checking belt tension.) Replace worn belts. Don't wait for them to let you down.

Add electric motor lubricating oil annually to the oil cups of the electric motor, just a few drops to ensure proper bearing lubrication.

Take care of the heart of your pneumatic system. Should it stop pumping, your entire system is "down." It won't stop pumping when properly maintained and checked. During power failure, the unit will be off. Should you loose pressure entirely, take advantage of compressor restarting to make a simple test. When the unit was new, it had an average "recovery" time, based on the number of minutes it would take for the unit to build up and cut off from zero pressure. To check the rings and valves in the pump, close the tank outlet valve and restart the unit, noting the time it takes to recover. Compare this with the control manufacturer's stated recovery time, provided in the compressor's operating and maintenance instructions. This will give you an idea of how new the unit is today. Reopen the valve to the system to reinstate controls operation.

CONTROLLERS AND THERMOSTATS

Should deviation from desired control points be noted, check the instrument's setpoint and calibration. When accessible, controller setpoints do sometimes get changed. Routine cleaning of the controller's levers, flexures, and pivot points can be accomplished with a very soft, fine brush, or low pressure air directed into the instrument from a small nozzle, such as a 5/32-in. barbed coupling. This will remove any accumulated lint, dust, or other airborne dirt sometimes encountered in equipment rooms. Check controller branch line output for proper buildup and bleeddown, and perform recalibration procedures for those devices demonstrating control point inconsistencies. Check for air leakage around the device where seals and diaphragms are installed.

RELAYS, EPs, AND PEs

If summer-winter or day-night lockout functions appear reversed, look for switching relays that are evidencing bleeding, sticking, or hanging.

On servicable models, check diaphragms and springs. On smaller ones designed for replacement rather than service, order new ones. EPs which should be energized will be warm, as evidence of their being "on." If cold, read coil continuity to examine the condition of the coil. An open circuit indicates a burned out unit. If continuity is good, be sure that the starter (or other device) to which it is wired is actually energized. PEs can be "pumped" to check for switch actuation with a meter across the terminals to permit "seeing" the circuit open and close.

DAMPERS AND ACTUATORS

Linkages on dampers should be kept lubricated to preserve smooth operation. Disconnect the actuator crankarm and manually operate the damper to feel any resistance, if you suspect that the damper is binding or not responding as it should. While loose, apply lubrication at the bearings and linkage assemblies, and continue to manually operate to note whether improvement is being accomplished. Note the exact connection point on the crankarm before disassembly, and reconnect it in the same place to preserve setup. Readjust it if damper closeoff does not occur completely when the actuator calls for it. Note the condition of the actuator and replace leaking diaphragms.

CONTROL VALVES AND ACTUATORS

Check the valve for close-off. Manually inspect heating coils that overheat when the valve is closed to see whether the let through is the fault of the control valve. When valves are leaking, replace renewable seats, after first verifying that the proper signal is being applied to the valve actuator when closeoff is supposed to occur. Again, check for leaks at the diaphragm of the actuator. Note any drippage or seepage around the stem of the valve, denoting a loose packing nut or worn packing. Apply the valve stem lubricant recommended by the control manufacturer.

Proper maintenance will work with you over the years to preserve your control system and save you operational dollars.

Index

Index